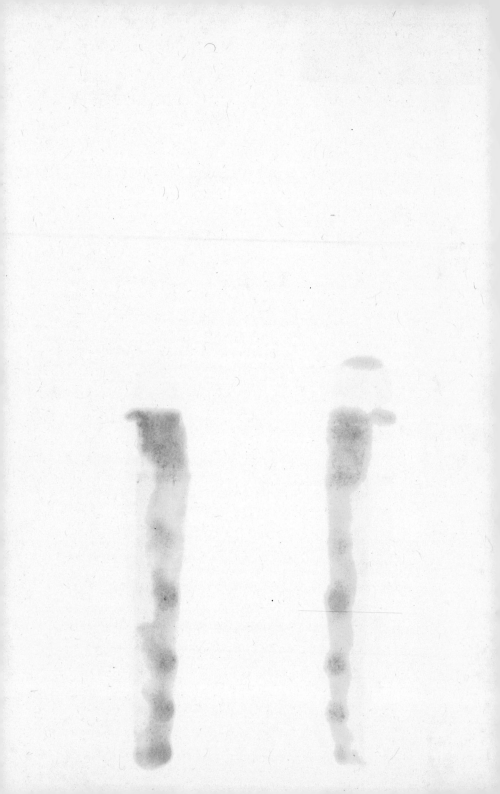

THE
COMMUNAL
CATHOLIC

THE COMMUNAL CATHOLIC

A Personal Manifesto

Andrew M. Greeley

A CROSSROAD BOOK

SEABURY PRESS • NEW YORK

For Mary Jule

The Seabury Press
815 Second Avenue
New York, N.Y. 10017

Printed in the United States of America

Library of Congress Cataloging in Publication Data

Greeley, Andrew M.   1928–   The communal Catholic.

    "A Crossroad book."
1. Catholics in the United States. 2. Sociology, Christian (Catholic) I. Title.
BX1406.2.G694   282′.73   75-43844   ISBN 0-8164-0299-X

Contents

Preface

This book is written with every deliberate intention to make trouble.

I am fed up.

On the one hand, I am fed up with the persistence of subtle and sophisticated nativism, or anti-Catholic prejudice, among America's cultural and intellectual elites. But I don't blame them so much. As one very distinguished foundation official put it to me, "Why do you expect us to give it up when you Catholics are just beginning to practice it?"

I am even more fed up with the self-hatred, the crypto-nativism and assimilationism of the Catholic elite—and more recently, with the official church whose pronouncements are now strongly influenced by the currently fashionable left chic. Does the left hate America? So must the United States Catholic Conference. Does the left warn of the dangers of pluralism? So must all the party-line Catholic journals like *America* or *Commonweal*. Does the left insist that we must turn to socialism in the post-Vietnam era? So do their pale Catholic imitators. Does the left decree that minority group spokesmen must have a veto on all public pronouncements? So does the committee that puts together the National Catechetical Directory. Does the left decide that the bicentennial must be an orgy of recrimination over the nation's failures—unmitigated by even the thought that something might have gone right in the United States? The USCC and its bureaucrats eagerly agree.

The Catholic elites are, as Msgr. Geno Baroni has pointed out, intellectually and morally bankrupt. They are twice ashamed—of being American and of being Catholic. In their repudiation of the American Catholic experience, they remind me of the trustees in the concentration camps who imitated storm troopers to the point of caricature.

To make matters worse, they are mostly dumb. They may claim to be an intelligentsia but they have precious little in the way of scholarly credentials and are utterly innocent of research data or experience. Morality and enthusiasm substitute for intelligence and evidence. They talk a lot, but they do not know what they are talking about.

All of this would not be a particularly great loss for anyone if there was nothing in the Catholic heritage which could make a contribution to the rest of American society. But when Harvard professor William Greenbaum writes a brilliant essay on the rise of pluralism, and Catholic voices decry too much ethnicity, one begins to wonder who the opposing teams are. And when economist E. F. Schumacher calls for an economic order which Jacques Maritain, Emmanuel Mounier, G.K. Chesterton, George Meany, and Richard Daley could endorse, but the official church goes on a liberation theology binge, one must ask what the hell is going on.

So I'm asking it. And I am frankly looking for a fight. I am disgusted by nativism and even more disgusted by the pale, sickly, self-hating ignorance of those who claim to be Catholic thinkers.

"Ah," say these types, "you're angry."

Damn right.

So they will spend all their efforts commenting on my anger and not responding to my positions, mostly because they are not perceptive enough to have the foggiest notion of what I am talking about.

But I do not intend to merely make trouble. I also intend to try to communicate with a new group of Catholics which is beginning to emerge and will continue to grow in American society. I call them the "communal Catholics" because they are strongly identified with the Catholic community but are rather uninterested in the organized church—and hence, like communal Jews, who vigorously identify themselves as Jews but barely show up in synagogue or temple on high holidays. If American Catholicism has any future at all, its best hopes lie with these communal Catholics who can transcend the foolishness of the present moment, in part because they have tuned it out. The communal Catholic, as we shall see in the first chapter, has begun to wonder if Catholicism, with its rich and varied tradition, has anything at all to say—which is not derivative from the current liberal chic—that might be pertinent to contemporary American problems.

Damn right it does.

Communal Catholics are more than just a focus around which to organize this book. They are both a product of the forces at work in the church and the larger society today and probably the single best hope the church has of responding creatively to the crisis it presently faces. Leadership, if it comes at all, will come neither from the official hierarchy nor from the self-appointed quasi-official intelligentsia; it will come rather from those who temporarily, if not permanently, have turned off both.

In the first section of the book, after describing the emergence of the communal Catholic, I deal with the problems these individuals must face as they search for their Catholic identity in an environment where they can no longer take the institutional church very seriously. In the second section, I turn to some of the resources which are available for the search of the communal Catholic out of his own heritage and tradition. Finally, I sketch the kind of church which I think the communal Catholic would find attractive—with the melancholy thought that they are probably going to have to create such a church for themselves with precious little leadership from either the hierarchy or self-anointed intelligentsia.

Three of the twelve chapters managed to find their way into print, in somewhat different form, before this book was put together. The introduction marked the tenth anniversary of the *National Catholic*

Reporter, the chapter on the vanishing one quarter originally appeared in the *Public Interest*, and the chapter on parochial schools appeared in *The New York Times*.

I wish to thank those who read all the chapters that make up this polemic—particularly William McCready and Ralph Whitehead—for their helpful comments, and Virginia Reich and Julie Antelman for typing and retyping the manuscript in its various developments. The book is dedicated to my sister Dr. Mary Durkin—not by any means a communal Catholic—on the occasions of her accession to the company of the learned and the publication of her first book. It will not, I think, be her last.

Andrew M. Greeley

CHAPTER ONE

The Emergence of the Communal Catholic

Predicting the future has always been great fun. It does involve, of course, a moderate amount of blasphemy because it represents a claim, however implicit, of being able to read the mind of God. Still, God apparently doesn't mind, and by the time the future arrives, most of those who have read predictions will not be around (for that matter, neither will the predictor) or will have long since forgotten what was so confidently prophesied.

There are, it seems to me, two general styles of forecasting. One is to try, as economists have done (with such notable lack of success recently), to project present trends into the future. "If things go the way they are now, then this is the way things will be." If there are enough variables in your model and a large enough memory storage in the computer, you can write all kinds of scenarios about what will happen if different variables are modified. This is a rather safe form of forecasting because with a sufficient number of variables and enough computer runs one will generate enough scenarios to cover every imagined possibility plus a few no sane person could ever imagine (which doesn't mean they won't occur). In the case of American Catholicism, computer model-building is impossible because there simply isn't enough data measuring changes over time to elaborate alternative scenarios. One must be content with saying very

hesitantly that, considering the factors the way they seem to be continuing, then the situation will be. . . . Such forecasting is a little bit
better than guesswork, but it is about all that can be done given the
strong resistance in American Catholicism to systematic and reg-
ularized data collection.

The alternative is to abandon all consideration of the present situation and describe the future as one would like it to be, which turns
projection into apocalypse or eschatology. Thus, for example, Ivan
Illich's article about the future of the priesthood, which appeared
some time ago in *The Critic,* is fascinating eschatology based on his
unquestionably sharp insight but supported by no available evidence
of any sort.

What I shall attempt in this chapter is mostly projection, but I will
cheerfully concede that there will also be some admixture of eschatology.

My central proposition can be stated simply:

In the next ten years Catholicism, *as an ecclesiastical institution* in
the United States, will continue in the course of its precipitous decline. At the same time, however, American Catholics, *as a community* in our society of pluralistic integration, will experience a
dramatic increase in healthy self-consciousness and self-awareness.

Part of the present problem of the American church is that a proposition such as the one stated in the previous paragraph doesn't mean
much unless one first lays out the conceptual tools that have been
used to build the proposition. By "ecclesiastical institution" I mean
the organized church: the hierarchy, the priesthood, the religious orders of women and men, and the various institutions which are administered by these groups of people—schools, orphanages, hospitals, charitable institutions, organizations of laity directly under
church control, as well as newspapers, magazines, and other forms
of communication with an official or quasi-official character. I also
include those subsidiary institutions that, while they are not directly

part of the organized church, exist mostly to service it—religious goods stores, newspapers, and magazines whose primary focus is the institutional church.

By the "Catholic community" I do not mean community in a theological sense ("people of God assembled in the Eucharist") or the social-psychological sense (as conveyed in that worst of all postconciliar nonsense cliches, "to build community"). I mean Catholics as a collectivity within the larger American population. The Catholic community in the sense I use it here is roughly equivalent to the "Jewish community" or the "black community." It refers to a populace rather than to an organized structure.

The difficulty in making any sense out of this distinction is that, of all the collectivities in America's system of pluralistic integration, the Catholic community is the one where the distinction between ecclesiastical institution and collectivity of people has been the least clear and distinct. No one confuses American Judaism with the organized rabbinate; no one confuses the black community with its ministerial associations. In both groups there is a long tradition of nonecclesiastical organizations and the members are considered valid spokesmen for the community both inside and outside of it. Rabbis and ministers have great influence, but there are other power centers within the collectivity that have an independent influence of their own, not necessarily in opposition to the religious institution but distinct and separate from it.

Within some of the American Catholic ethnic groups—particularly those of southern and eastern Europe—there are separate power centers, although they do not have nearly as much influence as the church. The Polish National Alliance, for example, in its origins and to some extent even today, represents a countervailing force independent of the church and only occasionally in direct opposition to it. But in the United States, there is only one organization which is unquestionably "Catholic" and that is the official church. How this came to be and whether it is the result of heavy Irish influence in the development of American Catholicism, are questions that are beyond

4 THE COMMUNAL CATHOLIC

the scope of this chapter. For our purposes, it is sufficient to say that the distinction between the Catholic church and the Catholic community is a very difficult one for most Americans—Catholic as well as non-Catholic—to grasp. Whatever the theologians have to say on the matter, the fact remains there is only one organized body which speaks for the Catholic community, and that is the church.*

Individual Catholics have made it in the business and political worlds, but they have left the role of official Catholic leadership and official Catholic concern to the institutionalized church. In years gone by, this division of labor may have been useful and efficient, and despite the protests of those who wish to have an autonomous role in lay leadership, most of the Catholic laity were perfectly willing to go along with the arrangement. One of the certain developments of the next decade will be that this distinction between institution and collectivity, which now may seem so strange, will be commonplace by the time Big Brother descends upon us in 1984. We will discover in the next decade that the continued deterioration of the church as an institution will have relatively little impact on Catholics as a social collectivity, and not much more on their religious affiliation and behavior. It *helps*, in other words, to have an ecclesiastical institution because in the long run you can't do without it. But however disastrous it may be for those who earn their livings and find their lives' fulfillment in servicing the institution, you can do without it very well, and the collectivity may still survive with a considerable level of religious commitment.

What do I mean when I say that the church as an institution will

*No one has yet attempted a serious and dispassionate study of fraternal organizations like the Knights of Columbus. My colleague Arthur Mann says that he has the impression this is one of the most important yet neglected aspects of American Catholic history, and that the Knights were in the antidefamation business several decades before the Jewish antidefamation organizations began their work. Whatever might be said of the Knights' past and the importance of their contribution (and I think it may be very substantial), no one at the present time would think that the Knights represent a distinct center of power within the church the way the Anti-defamation League or the American Jewish Committee do within the Jewish community.

continue to deteriorate? I do not mean merely that there will be a very low level of vocational recruitment, a continued decline in some forms of observable religious practice, and a further deterioration of the Catholic "marketplace" in books, magazines, and other religious goods. I am inclined to think that most of these declines will continue, but more importantly, the church as an institution will have less and less influence on the lives of people. National and international meetings of bishops, once front page news, will hardly be noticed by either journalists or the Catholic public. The election of a new pope, of course, will be a great event, but the shifting of power in the Catholic Conference of Bishops will barely be noticed. So what if we are delivered from Annas to Caiaphus and back to Annas? The image of the priest and nun, already badly deteriorated, will not improve; and even those Catholics who still have respect for the priesthood and the religious life will not take priests or nuns very seriously as a source for guidance even on religious matters. The various organizations which purport to speak for the priesthood and the religious sisterhood will continue to issue shrill pronouncements, but no one will be listening. Those intellectuals and journalists like Garry Wills and Wilfrid Sheed who either man the principal Catholic journals of opinion or interpret Catholicism for the rest of the American public will discover no one is much interested anymore. They will have an increasingly difficult time finding readers for their books and audiences for their lectures.

Finally, the "revivalists" (and I use the word in a nonpejorative sense), those movements in the church such as marriage encounter seminars and Pentecostalism which are brave attempts to restore the simple enthusiasms of a decade and a half ago, are almost certain to waste away simply because an increasing proportion of the Catholic population by 1984 will not have experienced the certainties of preconciliar Catholicism. From the National Conference of Catholic Bishops, to the parish Altar Society or charismatic group, from *The Wanderer* to the *National Catholic Reporter,* from *Cross-Currents* to Fatima devotions, the experience will everywhere be the same:

people just won't be interested anymore. There is a remote possibility that apostolic delegate Archbishop Jadot's "reform" (by appointing "pastoral bishops") may reverse this trend. I truly hope so, but with all due respect to Archbishop Jadot—and he is one of the most astute and adroit churchmen I have ever met—I fear that he may have come too late. I would very much like to be proved wrong.

The basic reason for this decline in influence had nothing to do with the success or failure of the Vatican Council, or with any of the other explanations that have been advanced to put some meaning into the traumatic crisis that the American Catholic institutionalized church is currently experiencing. Quite simply, what has gone wrong is we have been caught in two transitions: from Counter-Reformation to Ecumenical Age, and from the immigrant old neighborhood to the professional class suburb. We are forced to struggle through these twin changes with an almost total absence of ideas. No one is listening to the church as an institution anymore, not because of any crisis of faith or revolt against authority; no one is listening because the church as an institution in the United States today has nothing to say. The church has lost its influence in the Catholic community because it is almost totally innocent of ideas. In a literate community with dramatic change occurring, he who has no ideas has no influence.

The culture of institutional Catholicism—and by culture I mean the dominant ideas and styles of thought—is almost totally derivative. When the official spokesmen for the hierarchy, clergy, or lay elites wish to express something that passes for thought, they turn to others for words, phrases, and sentences. Depending upon who they are, they may take their inspiration from Holland, Germany, Latin America, or the currently fashionable and conventional wisdom of the American guilt-ridden liberal elite. Or they may use, in slightly modified form, the language of the traditional triumphal *stylus curiae*. I got into trouble a few years ago for saying the top-level leadership of the hierarchy was intellectually and religiously bankrupt. I will not broaden the charge: so is the top-level leadership of the presbyterate, the religious sisterhood, and the lay elite.

Thus, at a time when a number of non-Catholic writers are re-evaluating the Mary myth (men like Harvey Cox, Theodore Roszak, Lynn White), the American hierarchy issues a document on Mary which is nothing but a rehash of the dullest and most unimportant cliches of the desiccated maryology of two decades ago. Similarly, when the American hierarchy needed a description of the state of "evangelization" in the American church for the recent synod, they had one of their staff press agents put together a pastiche of cliches about American "malaise," "selfishness," and traditional episcopal concern about the evil influences of the secular world. That a number of Catholic elite journals applauded at least the first part of the statement, shows what sad shape those journals are in. Just leaf through the most recent four or five issues of *America* or *Commonweal* (once splendid and exciting journals) to discover how deadly dull and uninteresting they are. And if you want to know the latest strident cliche from the elected spokespersons (and the self-anointed consciences) of the clergy and religious, just read the editorial pages of last week's *New York Times, Washington Post,* or *Christian Century.* If you want to hear the currently fashionable and conventional wisdom of the liberal, you can find it stated much better and with much more solid documentation from secular journals and secular spokesmen. If all that is left of the institutional church is to echo either the slogans of the Counter-Reformation or the slogans of the contemporary liberal left, why should anyone bother to listen? Echos are never as clear as originals.

Will the Catholic church in the United States come to an end? It most assuredly will not—unless one is so foolish to believe that what the leaders and spokesmen of an ecclesiastical institution say has much impact on the religious faith of ordinary people. American Protestant denominations have flourished for years, decades, even centuries with their institutional organizations having far less impact on the ordinary congregants than the American Catholic church presently has. Still, there is no evidence that Protestant denominations are going out of business. A loss of influence by religious leadership may over the long haul—several generations—lead to massive apostasy. There is no sign, however, in any of the empirical evidence available, that Catholicism in the United States is moving in such a direction. People may not be going to church as often, and maybe aren't turning to their religious leadership for political, social, moral, and religious guidance; but that does not mean they have stopped being Christians or Catholics or, indeed, that they will disaffiliate in any formal way from the ecclesiastical organization which is still useful and even necessary at certain times in their lives. You can define yourself as a Catholic Christian and lead an exemplary Christian life and never know the name of your bishop, much less the name of the president of the National Conference of Catholic Bishops. You can be an intelligent and devout Christian without having heard of the *National Catholic Reporter,* much less subscribing to it.

Yet while the ecclesial institution deteriorates, the self-awareness and self-consciousness of the Catholic community improves as an ever increasing number of people begin to wonder quite explicitly what it means to be a "human" and religious Catholic in the United States. There are three factors, I think, which made such a development inevitable. The grandchildren and great grandchildren of the immigrants are now secure members of American society, no longer having to prove their Americanism to a hostile and suspicious host culture. Furthermore, there was a dramatic increase in educational achievement among Catholics. (In 1945, 14 percent of the Catholic population had attended college, and in 1974, the proportion had risen to 40 percent. In 1960, Catholics were 25 percent of the college graduates in the country, their exact proportion in the total population. They are now thirty-five percent of the college graduates. Catholics are therefore half again as likely to graduate from college as the national average.) The combination of educational achievement and economic success provides people with both the time and the security (financial as well as personal) to begin to ask themselves questions about the influences that have shaped who and what they are. Finally, the rediscovery of pluralistic integration, occasioned in great part by the black militancy of the 1960s, has made all Americans conscious of the fact that there is wide differentiation in the backgrounds which we come from. To understand one's own background may well be a necessary precondition for understanding the backgrounds of others. One may not like the rediscovery of pluralistic integration but its influence on the self-awareness of an ever interesting number of Americans is still an important cultural development.

In recent months I have been struck by the number of people I encountered whom I would describe as "communal Catholics." I believe that these people are the wave of the future, in part because some of them will surely have considerable impact on the Catholic community in years ahead but also, and perhaps more importantly, they are the first sign of a development that history and demography makes almost inevitable.

What is a communal Catholic? I would suggest that a communal Catholic is one committed to Catholicism and self-conscious in his attempt to understand the Catholic experience in the United States. He does not care much what the church as an institution says or does not say, does or does not do. He is committed to Catholicism as a collectivity and as a world view (though he reserves the right to interpret that world view to meet his own needs). But his expectations of the church as an ecclesiastical institution are minimal. Unlike some of his predecessors, he does not grow irate when the church fails to take a stand on the latest fashionable social issue, he doesn't much care because he isn't very confident that church leaders are well informed about such issues. Even if they did take a stand, he would not listen very seriously to what they say. However, he will turn to the church for sacramental ministry when it is needed, and he may deem that ministry to be needed very frequently in his life. He will not expect religious, social, moral, or human guidance from the church. He will admit that in principle it would be nice to have deeply spiritual and pastoral bishops, priests who would be holy men and effective preachers, and dedicated nuns. It would be nice to have intellectuals and journalists who did not parrot the latest conventional wisdom. But the communal Catholic's religious commitment and stand within the Catholic collectivity is quite independent of the intelligence, sensitivity, creativity, or spirituality of the leaders within the ecclesiastical institution. Communal Catholics are much more likely to be explicitly reflective and self-conscious about their Catholic heritage. No, I must say more. It is not merely that they are self-conscious about the heritage, they are—and this is astonishing (almost scary)—proud of it.

I do not detect in any of these communal Catholics the slightest trace of anger at the institutional church or their experiences growing up Catholic. They may laugh at the old monsignor, the pious superstitions of mother superior, the crazy things they heard in parochial school, bingo, or the terrible Sunday sermons; but unlike an earlier generation of Catholic intelligentsia, they apparently were not hurt by any of these experiences. Indeed, they seem to have an affectionate respect for the religious functionaries of their past. Mind you, they do not wish to see the past recreated, but they do not condemn it.

They seem at ease in their Catholicism. Some rarely show up in church and others receive communion several times a week. Some are not quite able to articulate what they believe; others become tongue-tied when the subject is raised; and still others will admit just now they don't know whether they believe anything. But they are all Catholics and do not intend to be anything else. As one man put it to me, "Right now, I think I'm still an atheist, but, damn it, I'm a *Catholic* atheist!" Or as one young woman said to me, "Of course I'm a Catholic. I'm not sure exactly what that means, but I couldn't be anything else." The communal Catholics, then, may still be engaged in painful, personal, and religious search, but they are not content with the posture of uncertain skepticism and near disbelief reflected by some of the official interpreters of Catholicism in the national secular journals. And whatever direction their religious pilgrimage may go, it is inconceivable that they would stop being

Catholic. This is, I submit, not merely a matter of ethnic loyalty but also a realization that the Catholic symbol system has so shaped their personalities that there is no way they can escape the influence of that shaping. Rather, they make peace with the Catholic symbol system and try to find some guidance from it for their personal problems.

I have already mentioned that they are proud of their Catholic heritage. I find such pride disconcerting because I have become so accustomed to the self-hatred and the perpetual inferiority complex which has been *de rigueur* for Catholic liberals the last several decades. The pride of the communal Catholics I know is neither militant nor belligerent; it is not like the arrogance of the church Berserk of a couple of decades ago. They simply think being a Catholic is a good thing, and on the whole, at least for them, it is better than being something else. When someone asks them why they are still Catholic, they look a little confused and may respond, "But why not?"

They are to a person religiously concerned. They don't much care who wins the election of the National Conference of Catholic Bishops or who is president of their priests' senate; but they are very much interested in figuring out what human life means, how to respond to the ambiguities, challenges, and poignancies of the human condition, how to articulate values to pass on to one's children, and, in some cases, how to convene a support group to share religious experience with and reinforce value transmission. They have opinions on the big issues which agitate the official church. They believe priests should be able to marry if they want, although they also respect their friends who are celibate. They have long since decided in favor of birth control; they tend to be against abortion and are ambivalent about divorce, which they don't like, but are aware of how impossible some marriages can get. They believe in marriage, are dubious about sexual permissiveness either as a way of life or as a revolutionary new phenomenon, and can see no earthly reason why women should not be ordained priests. But to tell the truth, they do not get very exercised about any of these issues, and are a little bemused why such questions seem so excessively important to the institutional church.

They are professionally competent. The ones I know are journalists, writers, politicians, administrators, research scholars, or some improbable combination of these roles. There is not a second-rater in the lot, not a single one who is employed as a token Catholic. They are among the best at what they do, and occasionally they are the very best of their generation. Perhaps the reason why they are so little involved with the institutional church is that they perceive, despite all the talk a decade and a half or so ago about competence, the church is still dominated by the untrained, or partially trained, amateur. When an enthusiastic, righteous young priest, filled with holy zeal for reforming the city, encounters a woman of his generation who knows the professional ins and outs, and ups and downs of urban administration, she may listen politely but might depart from the conversation with the thought that he may be a nice young man but terribly innocent and uninformed, someone who trades on his Roman collar as a cover for his ignorance.

The professionalism of these communal Catholics is so much a part of their lives that they simply cannot understand how it could be otherwise. They are offended by Sunday sermons, not so much because the content is either too radical or conservative, but because they are so bad. The main reason some of them stay away from weekly mass is the offensive amateurism of the sermon; and if they don't read the books that come out of Catholic publishing houses, then it is because the books are so frequently written by people whose intellect and powers of expression have never undergone the discipline of professional training.

The communal Catholics I know are hard to fit on any left-right ideological spectrum. They are skeptical of the conventional wisdom of both the right and left, and are more likely to be pragmatic technicians than enthusiastic idealogues. I can't think of a single Republican on my particular list, but then I don't know very many Republicans anyhow. I only know of one really enthusiastic McGovern supporter, and he had a very high place in the McGovern organization, although now he admits that McGovern was a disastrous mistake. Most of the others are as unwilling to take guidance from people who do their political thinking for them as they are from those who have traditionally done their religious thinking for them.

I doubt that any of them will ever become professional or official Catholics the way John Cogley was and the way many of the people in the *Commonweal* stable of writers still are. They will not become Catholic spokesmen, nor will they likely work for church organizations (though occasionally one may teach at a Catholic university). A career in, or adjacent to, the Catholic institutions has no appeal. It is not that they rejected such a possibility; they just simply never considered it seriously. Whether or not a professionally oriented and creatively intelligent ecclesiastical organization would have any appeal as an area of career commitment must be considered an academic question at the present time. But if a career of serving the church in an organizational capacity is not attractive, neither is one of criticizing it, interpreting it, or of being part of the official loyal opposition. Doubtless there will emerge some successors to the John Cogleys, the James O'Garas, the Daniel Callahans, and the Michael Novaks, but they will not come from among the communal Catholics I know. (More likely they will be people like Professor Roger Van Allen of Villanova, who recently seemed to express approval of Avery Dulles's idea that carefully constructed theological models are a form of "fence-sitting." The difference between Professor Van Allen and the communal Catholics I have encountered is as good a symbol as any I know to point out the difference between an ecclesiastical Catholic and the communal Catholic. Professor Van Allen's anguished cry for "more honesty" in the church would seem strange indeed to cool minded, hard nosed pragmatists who are much more concerned with competence and intelligence and much too realistic to expect much in the way of honesty in any human organization.)

But despite their lack of interest in the internal affairs, internal politics, and internal debates of the organizational church, the communal Catholics are each profoundly and deeply involved in a search for understanding what it means to be Catholic in America. Their search is open minded, open ended, respectful, sympathetic, and critical. For a few it is their primary professional concern; for others it is one of their main professional interests; and for most it is a principal concern of their lives though it may not fall within the scope of their professional skills and commitments. If they are not engaged in the present internal ecclesiastical debates, the principal reason is they do not find the categories and terms of these debates nearly as broad as their own interests. To argue, for example, about the popular election of bishops seems pointless to someone who is trying to understand how the Catholic communal ethic has influenced the development of urban government and may be able to influence a reform and renewal of urban government.

I have written of these communal Catholics as though they are lay men and women. Most of them are, but there are also some priests I know and one nun. In principle there is no reason a priest or a religious has to be an ecclesial Catholic, although it is perhaps somewhat more difficult for them to become communal Catholics because the culture they must spend so much of their time in is strongly ecclesial and not able to comprehend the possibility of another modality of Catholicism. In the ecclesial world view you can be a Catholic *for* or *against* the church, but the alternative that is offered is either committed ecclesial Catholicism or apostasy; ecclesial culture cannot comprehend how people can be committed to Catholicism both as a religion and a human collectivity with a unique and distinctive heritage and still be serenely indifferent to the ecclesiastical organization. A priest and a religious who in effect tries to straddle both worlds is caught in some cross pressures. The ones I know, however, seem able to manage it.

While they are very self-conscious in their search for insight and understanding, the communal Catholics have yet to emerge as a self-conscious, collective group within the church, and they may never do so. I have a stack of letters in my file from one communal

Catholic who vigorously insists on the need for a "Catholic School of Social Policy," which would surely be a rallying point for the communalists. In the January 1975 issue of *Concilium,* one of the most perceptive and sensitive communalists describes the ambiguities and the difficulties that those in his position experience. I have the sinking feeling that in most of the countries where *Concilium* is published people will not have the slightest idea of what he is talking about—neither, I fear, will a large number of ecclesial Catholics in the United States. Still, for those readers who think I am making it all up, the article in the January *Concilium* might make interesting reading. Then you will at least know the name of one communal Catholic.

What does this emergence of Catholic communalism mean *religiously?* I am not sure I know how to answer that question. Socially, the cultural and intellectual leadership will pass from the hands of the hierarchy and the clergy into the hands of those people whose principal concern is to criticize the hierarchy and the clergy, and are more or less indifferent to the behavior of both the ordained leadership of the church and those locked in dialogue with the ordained leadership. Over the long haul, such a shift will have a profound influence on the shape of American Catholicism, but it is, I submit, too early to even begin speculating about what such a change will mean. A mature, simultaneously sympathetic and critical self-awareness will make for more religious behavior on the whole. A person who stands at ease within his own religious tradition, needing to fight neither for it nor against it, will surely be much more self-possessed and self-assured in his personal and religious growth. It seems obvious such people will have increasing impact on both the Catholic community and, over the long haul, on the ecclesiastical institutions. How strong that influence will be and how long it will take to affect the ecclesiastical organization are questions which I cannot even pretend to answer.

Can the communal Catholics be organized? Surely it is not the time, and it may never be the time, to convene a national convention of them, although small, informal groups of them may meet intermittently. Do they represent a potential market for books, magazines, and newspapers? My guess is that there is an immense market out there; he who can find ways to serve it need have no fear of job security. Again, I cannot even pretend to know how such a market might be tapped or organized.

It must be clear that I like the communal Catholics. I feel that I share more of their ideas than I do those of the ecclesial Catholics I know. (I find it increasingly difficult to distinguish between letters from the chancery office and letters from the Priests' Senate. They are written in the same language, say the same things, are concerned with the same incredibly narrow issues, and produce the same mildly nauseous feeling in the pit of my stomach.) The communal Catholics feel no need to argue with me, preach at me, be threatened by me, hassle me, or patronize me. (If anything, the ones I know view me as an amusing eccentric, a role I find decidedly pleasant.)

But my liking for the communal Catholics is tempered by some reservations. Their affectionate nostalgia for what used to be is hard to reconcile with their cool indifference as the ecclesial organization crumbles into dust. So much of what they are was shaped by the organized church of the past that I think they ought to be much more concerned about trying to salvage the ecclesiastical structure before it becomes a hollow shell. In particular, they ought to be more concerned, it seems to me, about the dissolution of the parochial school system. Catholic schools are both ecclesial *and* communal, peculiarly enough. They are administered by the church organization, yet they produce most of the communal Catholics; and many, in fact, have their children in Catholic schools and would not dream of it being otherwise. Furthermore, as they search for an understanding of the American Catholic experience, many of them are beginning to say that the parochial school was *a* decisive if not *the* decisive component that made American Catholicism work for many years. I am thus surprised, and not a little frustrated, when these communalists shrug their shoulders as ecclesiastical authorities slowly dismantle the parochial school system. (The usual method is simply not to build new schools to meet shifting populations. In my own archdiocese, not a single Catholic school has been constructed in five years—but then, I am told, a new parish has not been opened in five years.) Maybe the communalists see more clearly than I; maybe the fight to reform and renew the ecclesiastical structure has already been lost, and there is nothing more to be done about it. But I think in this respect they are wrong.

So here are my prognostications for the next ten years:

1. Ecclesial Catholicism will decline. This is a bad thing, and I lament it.

2. Communal Catholicism will grow, expand, and become more self-conscious. This is a good thing, and I rejoice in it.

3. In the very long range I am confident that the ecclesiastical institution will be reshaped by the cultural forces that produced the communal Catholics and they in their turn will articulate, reinforce, sharpen, and develop. I do not know exactly what such a church will look like, but I think it will be an interesting one, and I would like to be around to see it. I do not expect to be.

But if the communal Catholics, their children, and grandchildren ever recall my name, I hope they remember I was on their side from the beginning.

section one   *Problems for*
the Communal
Catholic

CHAPTER TWO

The Vanishing
One-Quarter

A disturbing situation confronts the communal Catholic, namely that no one—Catholic or non-Catholic—knows very much about the one quarter of the population of this country which is Catholic. The communal Catholic knows in his gut that his heritage and the experience of his family are important. But if he wants to learn more about heritage and experience there is almost no place to turn. Catholic leadership, hierarchical and intellectual, and non-Catholic elites seem to agree that for all practical purposes, American Catholicism had neither a history nor a social structure which is worth knowing. If the communal Catholic wants to know more about his background, he is told that he doesn't have one. He is part of the quarter of the population which, as far as scholarship is concerned, has vanished.

And this seems to have happened largely over the past two decades.

In years to come, historians will shake their heads in disbelief over many of the events that occurred between 1960 and 1976. They may be shocked to discover that while Americans became concerned to the point of obsession about minority groups in society—Puerto Ricans, Chicanos, blacks, American Indians, Appalachian whites, homosexuals, prisoners, old people, etc.—virtually no interest was shown in the largest minority group in the population, Roman Catholics.

Defense attorneys pleading the case for our era before the tribunal of history might argue that there was no reason to be concerned about Catholics, because "the Catholic problem" was solved in 1960 when John Kennedy was elected to the presidency. The prosecuting attorneys might respond—after noting that Kennedy only won by a little over a hundred thousand votes—that the Catholic problem was not solved in the 1960s, and that even if it had been, the acculturation of the Catholic immigrants and their children, or at least the acceptance of the immigrants by the larger society, ought to have been a phenomenon of major importance to those who sought to understand the mechanisms and the processes of the American republic.

The facts of the case are striking.

ITEM: The basic *demographic* fact is that Roman Catholics constitute one quarter of the American population and are concentrated to a considerable extent in cities in the northeast and north central parts of the country, where they frequently comprise close to, if not in excess of, *one half* the population.

ITEM: The basic *historical* fact is that Catholics arrived as rather unwelcome immigrants—poor, uneducated, and ignorant of the language, customs, and styles of the new country. Furthermore, they were viewed by the larger society as superstitious, inferior, and frequently uneducable. Though they were let into American society (at least before 1920), they were not wanted.

ITEM: Hence, The basic *cultural* fact about the Catholic immigrants is that they were the objects of intense nativist prejudice, which denied Al Smith the presidency, almost denied it to John Kennedy, and, as I will argue in this chapter, has not yet dissipated.

ITEM: The basic *religious* fact to be noted about the Catholic quarter of the American population is that despite substantial pressure and social disadvantage, most Catholics have maintained an intense loyalty to the church of Rome, even though that loyalty gets more confused as the church itself gets more confused about what it stands for.

ITEM: The basic *socioeconomic* fact is that despite the barriers of history, culture, and religion Catholics have "made it" in American

society. Catholics under forty are as likely to be college graduates
and economically successful as are comparable American Protestants.* In addition, as the recent research of Lipset and Ladd has
demonstrated, Catholics have even begun to "make it" in the shel-
tered groves of the academy; approximately one fifth of the faculty
members under the age of thirty at elite colleges and universities are
Catholic. Catholics made up one quarter of the college population in
1960, and in 1972 their percentage rose to one third.

ITEM: The *political* fact that is most pertinent is that despite wide-
spread assumptions to the contrary, on most items of current political
and social interest the Catholic population is substantially to the left
of mainstream America. Irish Catholics are second only to Jews in
their scores on indicators of political and social "liberalism."

In brief, an extraordinary phenomenon has occurred in American
society in the last two decades, having a major effect on one quarter
of the population, and few people are even aware of the phenomenon, only a handful have tentative explanations for it, and the overwhelming majority of the American intelligentsia is not even re-
motely interested.

There is, of course, great interest in the Roman Catholic church.
While in the last decade it has not been very impressive as a church,
it has been splendid as theater, and for that has gotten front-page
coverage with greater frequency (with the recent exception of the
Episcopal ordination of women) than any other religious institution
in *The New York Times* and other papers. The news magazines, the
journals of opinion, and TV documentary shows all discovered
Catholicism around 1960, as revealed by *The New Yorker*'s mysterious agent, Xavier Rynne. John Kennedy, Pope John, Eugene
McCarthy, Daniel Berrigan, Alfredo Ottaviani, Francis Spellman,

---

*That is to say, Protestants whose geographic distribution is similar to that of
Catholics. It is inappropriate to compare Catholics with the general Protestant population because so many American Protestants are southern and rural that the general
"score" of Protestants on socioeconomic indicators is substantially lower than that of
the urban concentrated Catholics.

Terence Cooke, John Krol, James Shannon, Léon Suenens, Corita
Kent, Paul VI, Hans Küng, Theodore Hesburgh, Philip Berrigan,
Elizabeth McAlister, Ivan Illich, James Kavanaugh, Luigi Longo—
they are all fascinating copy. One can encounter, at any major university, professors in social science divisions who have constituted
themselves as experts on Catholicism because they religiously (one
should pardon the expression) read Xavier Rynne in *The New Yorker*
and Edward Fiske in *The New York Times*. Yet, when one gently
suggests that most of the change in the church's organization is not
so much the result of the Vatican Council as its cause, and that there
have been in the last twenty years profound, pervasive, and dramatic
changes in the Catholic *population*, which have had nothing to do
with Daniel Berrigan, John XXIII, or John Kennedy, these learned
social scientists look mystified. That changes could go on in the
Catholic population which influence the church as an organization far
more than the church influences the population flies in the face of
what most social scientists *know*, deep down in their consciousnesses, to be true about Catholicism.

The central fact is that the Catholics have "made it" in American
society. Such a fact is less a credit to Catholics themselves (though it
obviously does them some credit, one supposes) than it is to American society. For even though native Americans did not like Catholics
and were not especially pleased at their arrival, they nonetheless al-
lowed them into the country and permitted them to become part of it.
Catholics had to pay a price, and in some instance a heavy price, but
at least when they indicated willingness to pay, they were let in. This
is astonishing if one looks at the experiences of immigrants in other
countries. The plight of the "guest workers" from Italy and Yugo-
slavia in countries like Austria, Switzerland, Germany, and Sweden,
of the Algerians in France, and of the East Indians and Pakistanis in
England makes it quite clear that none of these allegedly enlightened
and progressive European societies is at all willing to tolerate ethnic
diversity. The guest workers are not generally permitted to become
citizens; if they are, it is only after many serious obstacles are over-

come. More importantly, they are not permitted to become part of the culture; in many cases they are not permitted to bring their families with them. The operating model for the guest worker is that he is the European equivalent of the *bracero,* who comes for a year or two to work in the host country and then returns to his own family and culture. His labor is wanted, but he and his family are not. He is a threat to the purity of the host culture.

Perhaps the enlightened and progressive European social democracies are not to be criticized too strongly for such behavior. After all, such exclusivism has been typical of most of human history, and suspicion of the foreigner—even if he lives just across the river—is much more typical than enlightened pluralism. But the point in a comparison of the American attitude towards cultural pluralism and, let us say that of the German or the Swedish, is that the comparison is rarely if ever made. I am unaware of a single American scholar who has pointed out, with perhaps some modest pride, that America did, after all, let the immigrants in, and however grudgingly, did permit them to become full fledged Americans—even on occasion, super-Americans. As the record of the human race goes in dealing with diversity, this is no small achievement.

The easy Marxist explanation for this is that the United States desperately needed unskilled workers as the economy expanded. But Sweden and Germany need unskilled workers today, too, which is precisely why they bring in Italian and Yugoslavian immigrants. A more sophisticated form of Marxism would contend that the rapid economic, technical, and territorial expansion of American society made it economically profitable for American capitalism to try to absorb the immigrant groups. But all this argument proves is that it was economically profitable to let the immigrants in. There were no particular economic reasons to let them move to the suburbs, or into the White House.

The truth of the matter is that we don't really know why a country, which until 1820 was almost purely Anglo-Saxon (and Scotch-Irish), was able in the course of a couple of decades to become one of the

most pluralistic societies the world has ever known—so pluralistic
that one might guess that Thomas Jefferson and James Madison
would have feared for the country's survival if they had known it was
going to happen. Nor do we have any clear idea why, despite the
tremendous diversification of American society in the middle and
later years of the nineteenth century, there has been relatively little
violence as the various groups in American life adjusted to one
another. There has been only one Civil War, and that was fought between essentially two Anglo-Saxon groups. In other words, if one
wishes to understand the relative success of American pluralism, the
acculturation of the Catholic population ought to be a fascinating and
informative test case.

My own hunch is that the native Americans became pluralists in
spite of themselves, because when the immigrants arrived on the
shore the native Americans were caught in an ideology which legitimated pluralism. It took almost a century before that ideology could
be overcome to the extent of barring further immigration. Nativism
triumphed in the immigration legislation after World War I, but its
triumph came much too late.

Much of the writing on the formative years of the American republic stresses the need to create an overarching social structure that
could take account of the geographic and economic diversity of the
various states. But if one reads the documents of the time, one also
becomes aware that the states were also denominationally diverse,
and that the founding fathers had to cope with a Congregationalist
New England, a Quaker Pennsylvania, an Episcopalian Virginia,
and a Free Church Georgia. The country was indeed denominationally pluralistic before it became politically pluralistic. The republic
established structures flexible enough later to include Boston Con-
gregationalists and Unitarians, Virginia Anglicans, Georgia
Methodists and backwoods Baptists; it was ill equipped both ideologically and structurally to say "no" when Irish Catholics arrived on
the scene. And once you had let in Irish Catholics, it was too late to
refuse the Poles and the Italians. The immigrants might have been

"wretched refuse," but they came and were let in. The "American dilemma" that Gunnar Myrdal saw in white attitudes towards blacks was merely a specification of a larger American dilemma: native Americans did not particularly like diversity, but their ideology gave them rather little option in the matter.

The official model of the Americanization process held that the individual immigrant and his children and grandchildren learned the language, went to school, worked hard, and eventually became "as American as anyone else." But the official model ignored the fact that the social mobility for the Catholic population has been a group mobility. The Germans, the Irish, and now, more recently, the Italians and Poles, made it into the upper-middle class as collectivities. And that ethnic and cultural diversity continues to flourish in the upper-middle-class suburbs; the Irish are still Irish, Italians still Italian, Poles still Polish.

Individual effort flourished within a context of very important group processes. First of all, there was the "internal mobility pyramid." One can become a success in American society, as sociologist Peter Rossi has observed, by serving the members of one's own constituency not merely as a politician but as a doctor, a lawyer, a dentist, a psychiatrist, an undertaker, a construction contractor, or a clergyman. While it is possible, as sociologist Norbert Wiley has pointed out, to get in the mobility trap—the Italian surgeon who makes it as the number one surgeon in the Italian community has little prestige in the non-Italian medical profession—even those who are caught there enjoy considerable economic success. The Mafia don or the corrupt Irish politician may not be able to get his daughters into the elite debutante ball, but his home, automobiles, and clothes will compare favorably with those of a native American aristocrat. And from their point of view, that may be all that matters. Secondly, there are in the large cities networks of such client-professional relationships. The Italian doctor sees an Italian lawyer when he wants legal advice; both of them have an Italian contractor to build their expensive suburban homes; and all of them vote for an Italian political leader to represent the interests of their community at city hall or the statehouse. Thus an exchange of goods and services goes on within the religio-ethnic collectivity which has a multiplier effect in contributing to the economic well-being of the community. Finally, there is the process of group conflict, symbolized by the struggle for political jobs, but which also includes conflicts over homes, neighborhoods, schools, jobs in education and industry, and in the churches. Again, what is astonishing is not the fact that this group conflict has gone on but that it turns into violence so rarely. Apparently, a whole series of rituals and protocols has been devised which enables American groups to carry on their conflicts at the level of rhetoric and to work out adjustments and accommodations which are more or less responsive to their respective powers in the context in which they are interacting.

But there is much that the ordinary American Catholic has had to give up in this process. The poetry, music, wit, mysticism, and passion of Celtic culture at its best has been lost by most of the American Irish. Similarly, the cultural riches of the other ethnic communities are either lost or still locked up within the ethnic neighborhoods and are not shared with the rest of society, in part because the nativist American doesn't think there are any riches in the ethnic communities and in part because the ethnic communities are afraid to share them with the rest of the society for fear that they will be ridiculed. The example of the American Jews, who have made immense contributions to the common culture, has not been successfully imitated by other groups, with the possible more recent exception of the blacks. The Irish, and probably the Germans, have abandoned their folk heritage; the Poles and the Italians and the other eastern European groups keep theirs carefully hidden. This is unfortunate it seems to me, for all concerned.

The Catholic ethnics have not stopped being Catholic ethnics. Our research data would indicate, however, that to a considerable extent they are ethnic in an implicit and frequently unconscious way. Behavior characteristics, attitudinal constellations, relational styles persist without many Catholic ethnics being aware that their behavior is different from that of others in the society. This forced repression of diversity is a loss both for the people involved and for the rest of the country. The present writer can hardly be optimistic about any dramatic changes in this area. When *The New York Review of Books* becomes as enthusiastic about Polish-American writers as about black-American writers, then the new fashion of cultural pluralism ought to be taken seriously indeed—but not until then.

The problem for Catholic intellectuals is much more serious, because the intelligentsia by its very nature cannot, like most of the rest of the Catholic population, spend most of its time with its "own kind of people." It must interact with mainstream intelligentsia if it is to achieve any prestige at all. If it is to be accepted by mainstream intelligentsia, it must, if anything, overacculturate. Just as rank and file American Catholics had to become superpatriots, so Catholic intellectuals who wish to make it into the mainstream must become almost caricatures of the ideal types of American intelligentsia. Being a Catholic is no longer an obstacle to acceptance among intellectual elites so long as you are the "right kind" of Catholic—not too pushy, not too militant, and, above all, not too Catholic (the functional equivalent of the light skinned Negro of a couple of decades ago).

The anti-Catholicism of the upper academy is subtle and frequently unconscious, but it is pervasive nonetheless. I recently heard it seriously argued at a national symposium that while the absence of blacks and women from the upper-level faculty positions at the great universities was a sign of discrimination, the absence of Catholics was not, because Catholics were in fact intellectually inferior. Nobody in the audience stirred in the slightest at such an incredible assertion. Younger Catholic scholars, almost by sheer weight of numbers, have made it into the academy, and, as data from the recent Carnegie research on college faculty indicate, are publishing articles and obtaining tenure in the same proportion as are Protestants. The academy can heave a sigh of relief. Catholics have finally become

bright enough and intellectual enough to merit prestige appointments, deanships, chairmanships, and university presidencies at secular institutions. But the Catholic intellectual is not only required to
be something less than committed to his Catholicism if he wants full
acceptance; he would also be wise not to become too concerned
about the explicit study of Catholic matters. He will probably be dis-
inclined to do this, in any case, because it was painful and took considerable emotional stress and strain to break out of the Catholic subculture and move into the larger society. When someone suggests to
him that there is something in that subculture that might be worth
analyzing and interpreting for the rest of society, he is not particularly disposed to take such advice seriously. Thus, among the official
American Catholic intelligentsia, only Michael Novak has shown
much concern about the new interest in ethnicity and cultural
pluralism, and he is not altogether willing to admit that the Irish are
ethnics. When you have just left the ghetto behind, it is difficult to
believe that you ought to go back into it to administer a questionnaire
or to write a novel that implies there might be something good going
on there.

What has happened, then, is that one quarter of the population has
disappeared. It is not necessary to ask why it may be underrepresented in some parts of academea. There is no reason to raise any
question about the possibility of the persistence of bigotry. Nor is it
worth asking what one might learn from the experience of the
Catholic ethnic groups that might be pertinent to more basic issues of
pluralism and diversity in American society. Finally, when someone
does step out of line and suggests that the neglect of the Catholic
phenomenon is passing strange, he is dismissed as somebody trying
to be "divisive" or "particularistic."

A Catholic can be president of the United States—indeed, a
Catholic can even be president of Columbia University, which is as
everyone knows a more important and more difficult task. Catholics
can make money, live in the suburbs, and even belong to most of the
clubs and get into most of the debutante balls in American society.

And for all this they should be grateful, one supposes. If their ancestors had come as strangers into most of the other countries of the
world, they wouldn't have progressed nearly as far nor as rapidly as
they have in the United States. Someday, it may even turn out that
what has happened to them and what they have done will be taken
seriously by those who shape America's elite culture. Then perhaps
even Professor Galbraith will be baffled by the absence of Catholics
on the Harvard faculty.

CHAPTER THREE

The Weaknesses of
American Catholicism

Not only does he not know what the Catholic experience has been,
the communal Catholic is hard put to say what Catholicism is. He has
the gut feeling that being a Catholic is a good thing; he certainly does
not want to be anything else, and could not contemplate either conversion or apostasy. The religious symbols of his childhood seem
important and he doesn't want to give them up, but he doesn't know
quite what they mean either. He wants to pass these symbols on to
his children, but how do you hand on symbols whose importance you
know, but whose implications you are hard put to express?

The problem then is one of ideas.

The fundamental crisis of the American church at the present time
is not structural, it is not sexual, it is not even in the primordial sense
of the word religious; it is *theoretical*. By theory I do not mean
abstract and unimportant ideas. I mean rather the goals, the values,
the models, and the basic assumptions implicit in everything that a
given group of human beings do. Every man needs a theory to interpret and order the phenomena that impinge on his consciousness, and
every human group needs a theory to justify its existence, to explain
its purposes to outsiders and new members, to underwrite its stan-
dard procedures and methodologies, and to motivate its members to
work toward the goals of the organization. That we American

Catholics are so little conscious of the theoretical dimensions of our behavior is no proof that we do not have theories. When we are told that we have theorized all along, we are as astonished as the character in the French comedy who was shocked to learn that he had been speaking prose.

The old theory was a mixture of post-Tridentine garrison Catholicism and American immigrant Catholicism. It stressed loyalty, the certainty and immutability of answers, strict discipline, a comprehensive Catholic community, suspicion of the world beyond the church, the avoidance of the reexamination of fundamental principles, and clearly defined models of behavior that were appropriate for the various levels of the church's structure. One can illustrate the nature of this theory by saying that it left little doubt as to what was inappropriate behavior either for the parish priest or for the layman. The priest taught in school, said mass, heard confessions, visited the sick, buried the dead, prepared young people for marriage, moderated parish organizations, tried to straighten out "bad" marriages, tried to reclaim "fallen away" Catholics, provided some sort of minimal instruction for those who were going to public schools, spent his day off with clerical classmates, made sure that somebody was always on call in the rectory, and if it was a particularly progressive parish, greeted the people in the back of the church after Sunday mass. The good Catholic layman went to mass and communion every Sunday (and sometimes even daily), contributed to the support of the parish, sent his children to parochial schools, was active in parish organizations, respected the leadership of his pastor, carried the rosary in his pocket, was faithful to his wife, and tried his best not to practice birth control.

I am not necessarily being critical of these models. In the post-Tridentine immigrant church, simple, clearcut, easily memorized models of behavior may very well have been appropriate. All things considered, one must make the historical judgment that the American church responded successfully to the challenge of the immigrant years. While the models of that period are no longer relevant, it is cheap, superficial, and arrogant to make fun of the past not from its own perspectives but from ours.

The assumptions underlying such models were unexamined and frequently unexaminable. One followed models of behavior, one did certain things and did not do certain other things becuase this was the behavior expected of Catholics. The reasons for the behavior were largely extrinsic. We may have given lots of reasons, but they were suasive and not decisive. Priests remained single because that was the Catholic way. Catholics did not elect bishops because the election of church leadership was the Protestant way. We didn't practice birth control because it was forbidden; we didn't enter into mixed marriages because they were against church law. Priests never asked what the role of the priest was because that role was clearly laid out by canon law and rectory custom. The whole set of beliefs, roles, and practices were all tied very closely together, and they were justified, for the most part, in terms of extrinsic loyalty to the church, not in terms of their intrinsic rationality. The theories, then, of pre-Vatican Catholicism were implicit, unexamined, and presumed to be unchangeable. One did not need to ask what a priest would be doing twenty years from now because he would be doing the same things he was doing now and the same things his predecessors did twenty years before. And he did them because that was what the church expected a priest to do. There was, of course, a theoretical difference between keeping a mistress and wearing a tie when one came down the front steps of the rectory, but both kinds of behavior for most of the clergy most of the time were equally unthinkable.

The approach of the church to theory served rather well at a time when most Catholics were uneducated immigrants, striving simultaneously to keep their faith and earn a place in American society. The grave weakness in such a rigid and inflexible theory was that if any piece of it fell into question, the whole structure would be open to doubt. If you began to examine one assumption or one aspect of a model, then everything would be examined. It hardly needs to be said at this point that the reforms of the Vatican Council began such a chain reaction of examination.

Such is the "meat on Friday theory" of the present condition of American Catholicism. Whatever we may have said about fish on Friday being merely a matter of ecclesiastical discipline, it was nonetheless a critically important symbol in the lives of most American Catholics. Once you demolish that symbol, everything else that was linked with it in the model of appropriate Catholic behavior was called into question. Similarly, if one seriously intended to prevent the present crisis in the priesthood, one would have had to act very early to head off the questioning of even the most simple regulations and assumptions. In other words, if every man who refused to use the pall in the appropriate fashion at mass in the early 1960s had been excommunicated, we would have a much more stable priesthood today. Once you permit questioning of even small parts of your tightly linked, extrinsically supported theoretical structure, the whole thing begins to crumble. Logically, there may be no connection between discarding the pall and seeking a wife, but psychologically, once one immutable rule is broken, all the others are vulnerable.

The reexamination of the whole range of our theoretical assumptions would have been a painful experience under the best of circumstances, but much chaos could have been avoided if we had been able to prepare for the transition by rethinking the grounds for our assumptions before the crisis came. However, the trouble with a theoretical posture supported by extrinsic authority is that there does not seem to be a good reason for a constant updating of the theory's rationale. One did not really have to think through the implications of the Freudian evolution for a Christian theory of sexuality so long as one could get away with forbidding birth control on the grounds that the church forbade it. Nor did one have to update one's own theoretical justification of ecclesiastical celibacy so long as the only argument really needed was that the church doesn't permit its priests to marry. One did not have to think too seriously about the implications for one's Christology of New Testament criticism so long as it was possible to keep clergy and laity away from New Testament criticism by telling them that they couldn't read it. One did not have to justify the frequently arbitrary exercise of authority by pastors and bishops so long as no one bothered to inquire in what precise sense bishops were thought to be successors of the apostles.

Pragmatism is a good thing, but to build a *new* American Catholic theory we must first discard the *narrow* and *militant* pragmatism so typical of the American church. Many priests, religious, and laity grow angry when someone appears on the scene, raises theoretical questions, suggests new issues, and departs without clear, concise, and easily programmed answers. As one irate pastor put it, "What the hell do you mean by coming here and disturbing us with your damn fool questions? We've got practical problems to solve in our parishes, and what we expect from a sociologist is solutions to those problems!" To make matters worse, narrow pragmatism is an excess of what is one of the unique virtues of the American Catholic church. We are without doubt the best organizers, administrators, and operators in the Roman Catholic world.

But a narrow pragmatism is really not pragmatic at all. He who cannot look beyond next fall's lecture series, or next Sunday's sermon, or next week's inquiry class, or next Friday night's discussion group will not have available the imaginative and creative resources required to do even a good job at the sermon, the discussion group, or the inquiry class. Still, the "how to do it" mentality is dominant. Unfortunately, during the last decade there have been prophets wandering all over the camp with the prepackaged programs, the magic answers to be applied in every parish, Newman Center, school, and CCD series in the country. Kerygmatic catechetics, salvation history, socially relevant sermons, ready-made prayer programs—they have all sold like hotcakes. At least for a year or two until it is discovered that however wonderful they sounded on paper the work of the local ecclesiastic only begins when he opens the mail—he still has to apply them to his own context. And it is precisely in that application that imagination and creativity, so often lacking in the narrow pragmatist, becomes indispensable.

Yet they ask, "What difference does Robert Heilbroner or Erich Fromm make to my parish, my Newman Club, my school, my adult

education program? Indeed, who the hell are those people? Most of
my people have never heard of them." Perhaps not. But how many
of those engaged in pastoral work would argue that questions of marital sexuality, the life crisis of the middle years, religious experience,
the transmission of values to one's children, living with those who
are culturally different from us, and confidence about the future of
the country and the human race are not pertinent problems on the
minds of substantial numbers of their congregations? These concerns
are not limited to the well educated. They may articulate them more
easily. They may not know who Heilbroner and Fromm are, but I
simply do not believe that the less well educated are either unaware
of or unconcerned about the questions of the nature of human nature
or of living in a complex, pluralistic society, or of passing on values
to their children, or of coping with the dreary angst of the middle
years. The pastoral worker who told me that his people are not concerned about these things is revealing how little he knows them. Of
course it will take imagination and ingenuity to see how these major
cultural strains can be responded to in that small segment of time
and space which is a parish, a school, a Newman Center, a CCD
program. And of course one will have to abandon the quest for simple, prepackaged programs. I can tell no one else how to do it.

Closely related to narrow pragmatism is the shallowness of
American Catholicism. For every problem there must be an answer,
for every issue there must be a stand, for every injustice there must
be a villain. One is either an optimist or a pessimist; a conservative or
a liberal; an old-fashioned Catholic or a postconciliar Catholic.
One's positions on issues must be consistent: if one is a postconciliar
or liberal Catholic, then one must be for birth control, against clerical
celibacy, for abortion, against elaborate liturgy, for ecumenism, and
against maryan devotion. One must also be enthusiastic about Harvey Cox, Karl Rahner, the grape and lettuce boycotts, the fight
against Farah pants (now happily won), women's liberation, premar-
ital sex, CCD instead of Catholic schools, the Berrigan brothers (until about a year or so ago), Dom Helder Camera, John Cogley, and

Charles Davis. One was also expected in past years to be excessively enthusiastic about the cursillo movement, sensitivity training, Catholic radicalism, liberation theology, Pentecostalism, and most recently, Key '73. It was also *de rigueur* to be passionately enthusasistic about Ivan Illich and Paolo Freire.

Granted that knee-jerk liberalism has never been more fashionable in the United States than it was up to the McGovern election disaster, it still must be said that a substantial number of Catholic clergy, religious, and involved laity have outdone the rest of the country in the skill and speed with which their knee reflexes work. As one might have expected, knee-jerk conservatism is also beginning to come into its own. Just as the Catholic liberals begin to lose their energy and self-confidence, having endured the National Association of Laymen and the National Federation of Priests' Councils for a number of years, we must now prepare ourselves to endure the Catholic United for the Faith and the Consortium Perfectae Caritatas. (Any group which uses the label "perfect charity" to describe itself is in trouble to begin with.)

What one fails to see in all this passionate eagerness to take stands on issues is the slightest awareness that the world is painted in other hues than darkest black or purest white. Shadings, ambiguities, nuances, complexities—these are as absent from the world view of the enthusiastic supporters of Cesar Chavez as they are from that of the most vigorous defenders of the Respect for Life movement. Now it so happens that I am appalled by abortion and impressed with Chavez, but I do not believe that Cesar is infallibile or that his cause should be identified totally and completely with the cause of Christianity; nor do I believe that the rigid, doctrinaire strategy of the Respect for Life movement is likely to win many allies. But the point is not my stand on abortion or the farmworkers, but rather that in the enthusiasms of both sides one sees precious little concern for anything else but the mindless repetition of slogans.

The quintessential slogan mouthed ad nauseam in enlightened Catholic circles is "the third world." Any cause, idea, movement, panacea that is fortunate enough to be identified with the third world is automatically assured of support. It is toward the third world that we tired old northern hemisphere types better look for virtue, wisdom, and expiation from our guilt as oppressors and victimizers. Never mind that much of what passes for third-world theology is a pathetic mixture of vulgar Marxism and quotations from conciliar documents and quite innocent of economic, sociological, or even empirical, data. Just as at one time we were expected to bend our knee in adoration before the worst sort of foolishness if it came from a black man, we are now expected to offer similar hyperdulia to all third world theologians as soon as they walk into the room.

But what is the third world? Is it Singapore, the cleanest city in the world with the second highest per capita income in Asia? Is it Japan with its fantastic gross national product? Is it Thailand with full employment and a thriving economy based on the exportation of rice? Is it Malaysia with an equally thriving economy based on oil palms and rubber? Are the Indians third world in India but not in General Ahmin's Uganda? Is India itself, with more natural resources than Japan and a population expanding out of control, third world in the same sense that Mexico is? Is Ireland, still occupied by a foreign army after a millennium? Are the Arab oil sheiks, whose price gouging may accelerate famine in the Indian subcontinent, to be covered with the sacred mantle of the third world? What about Argentina, rich in natural resources but unable for more than three decades to organize itself politically? What about Brazil with the second highest growth rate in the world? What about Chile, whose minority socialist government proved itself—despite all the advice from the liberation theology types—quite incapable of building a broad national consensus among a politically sohpisticated population? Is Uruguay third world, once the most stable and affluent of democracies, and now deteriorated into chaos because of the failure of its leadership? And the nonwhite colonies within the Soviet Union, Ubzekstan and Kahsakstan, which were added to the Russian empire about the same time India was added to the British empire, are these so-called autonomous Soviet republics part of the third world? Is Venezuela, which was able to have democratic elections and relatively peaceful changes of power, with its immense oil wealth in the same third world category as neighboring Peru, so short of natural resources and even shorter of democratic skills? One could go on, but I think the point is made.

As a symbol and a slogan the term third world may have some uses. As a serious tool for responsible analysis and programming, it is an utter failure. It eliminates completely the complexity, the diversity, the heterogeneity among the non-North Atlantic nations. Anyone who is serious about doing anything more than talk must drop the category third world and begin to consider the specific problems of the *individual* nation or region one is discussing.

It is impossible to discuss the third world with those who throw at me the slogans, "exploitation," "oppression," "victimization." Once these words are uttered the discussion is terminated; any attempt to raise questions about specific issues in specific countries or regions is ruled out of court. I suspect that many third world enthusiasts have very little idea of the economic, social, and political particularities of the different parts of their third world. Nor do they seem interested in acquiring knowledge about these particularities. It is not merely that their thought lacks sophistication and depth; they are not even aware of the necessity or the possibility of specification and depth as characteristic of thought.

One could make a strong case for the necessity of a group of superbly trained Catholic specialists in international economics (including such mundane aspects of economic development as tropical agriculture and animal husbandry). Such specialists, securely committed to their faith and trained in their own disciplines, could make an important contribution to the solution of world economic problems. They might also create a bridge between religious and economic thought. There was a time in the old days of the Catholic Action movement when the training of such religiously committed professional specialists was high on the agenda of many American Catholics, but somehow respect for professional competence got lost in the mindless enthusiasms of the last decade. The person who raises issues of economic complexity finds himself written off as conservative or as an exploiter. Slogans and ideological symbols like the third world are fine for stirring up enthusiasm, but they are useless as guides to practical programs and intelligent social intervention. One reads Alvin Toffler's *Future Shock* and becomes an expert on the problems of technology; one plows through Paulo Freire's turgid ideology and becomes well informed on the economics of developing nations; one takes a course or two in counseling, or even acquires an M.S. in the subject, and becomes a trained psychiatric practitioner; one reads Mary Daly and becomes a specialist on the problems of women in the church and in the modern world; one glances through *The God I No Longer Believe In* and knows all there is to know about contemporary issues of fundamental theology.

We are plagued by amateurism. It used to be that anyone who wore a Roman collar or a veil was thought qualified to teach college theology. We now apparently know better than that, but the amateurism persists. You can take a summer course in counseling and set yourself up in business as a psychotherapist. You can be in Latin America for a year and emerge as an expert on world food problems. You can go to a meeting and read an article in *The New Yorker* and pontificate about multinational corporations. You can spend a few months at a European catechetical center and come back to revamp a diocese's religious education program. You can attend a conference on poverty and return with a plan to remake American society.

The National Conference of Catholic Bishops seems especially disposed to such amateurism. Its report to the Synod of Bishops was drafted by its staff's public relations man. Its bicentennial discussion guide was put together by a group of uninformed mediocrities (with the exception of one brilliant essay by theologian David Tracy). Its book on poverty was written by an educational director who cheerfully admits that he is not an economist. When bishops engage in such behavior you can hardly blame parish priests for not preparing their sermons.

We hire professionals to build our churches, to provide our legal counsel, to do our accounting, and (sometimes) to invest our funds. We would not want a church designed by someone who had taken one course in architecture or our funds invested by someone who went off to the library and looked over a few books. We would not ask a public relations man to make sure that we were meeting the IRS tax requirements for our employees. We don't turn our printing jobs over to some kids in a basement with a press. On the contrary, the layout in the NCCB books is professional, only the content is amateurish.

When it comes to *ideas* we are content with the second-rate, the derivative. We are suspicious of the professional thinker or scholar. We prefer the pious but untrained Jesuit expert on international relations to Daniel P. Moynihan who, unbelievably, has never been asked of his church to do anything but hand in his Sunday envelope. In the depths of our hearts we believe that when it comes to ideas, expertise, and analytic insight, the amateur is superior to the professional.

Furthermore, we have absolutely no respect for our own experience and our own people. We are devoid of self-awareness and historical understanding. We delight in celebrating our own failures, in particular those of the Catholic schools. Yet historians of the future will argue that the implicit decision made in the 1960s to curtail the construction of Catholic schools and new parishes turned out to be the worst disaster in the history of American Catholicism. For whether the schools were educationally effective or not (and my empirical evidence persuades me that they were), they were really the center of the parish community. Once we began to produce parishes without schools we began to produce parishes without community. The Catholic schools were one of the unique accomplishments of the American church, and we wrote them off in an enthusiasm to find new and better techniques and in an orgy of self-hatred.

I belong to a group of Catholic urban experts in Chicago—an underground group without name or explicit purpose. At a recent meeting every one of the very sophisticated specialists around the table agreed that the decision not to build parochial schools in the suburbs was the worst mistake American Catholicism has ever made. None of these people had vested interests in parochial schools, and all were speaking from the viewpoint of their professional specialties. We had a good thing going for us and we never even bothered to try to understand why it might be good.

And we so delight in stereotyping and scapegoating our own people. They are, as Monsignor Rice argued with me not so long ago, racists and bigots. We have failed to teach them Catholic social principles, or, as yet another Catholic liberal commented at a meeting of urban ministry types at the University of Notre Dame, "We have to be ashamed of our own people." There is considerable evidence, of course, that the Catholic population is less racist than other elements in the population of the northeast and north central parts of the country. There is also evidence that the Catholic population overwhelmingly supported every liberal social reform in the last fifty years. But evidence is not really the point. The precious elitists who were involved in the urban ministry had to feel morally, intellectually, and religiously superior to the poor, simple Polack or Dago who lives in an ethnic parish and doesn't read the *Commonweal* or *The New York Times*. What in the world could we ever learn from the ethnic or the ethnic parish that would have any pertinence at all to religious and social problems in American life?

Not a single journal is ready to devote any space to a sympathetic though critical reevaluation of the meaning of the American Catholic experience. It is not necessary to reexamine that which by a prior definition is worthless, and it is not necessary to understand the incredible change that has occurred in the Catholic population socially, economically, and religiously since 1945 when they have already been written off as superstitious, priest-ridden bigots. Besides, what pertinence could such bishops as Gibbons, Ireland, Spaulding, Keene, Carroll, and England possibly have for our own time? Much better to read Mary Daly.

One must also say (and here I engage in some painful honesty) that like all self-hating minority groups we are not very good at standing by our own kind. Priests, religious, or laymen who somehow step out of the ranks to do something unusual or extraordinary are likely to be the victims of endless effort to cut them down to size or to destroy their character. The shabby treatment by the Jesuits, for example, of John Courtney Murray, Gustav Weigel and Joseph Fichter will be a blot on the distinguished record of that community, as will their treatment of Dan Berrigan in his early days when that story is fully revealed. This peculiar need to cut up one's own became pathetically obvious to me when I once toured Maryknoll mission stations in Asia with my friend and colleague, Maryknoller Gene Kennedy. I was used to the treatment I got in my own archdiocese, but it was interesting to be able to watch the same thing being done to someone else from the outside. The reaction to Kennedy was one of scarcely veiled suspicion. What *exactly* was he doing? What sort of work was he in? What purpose was his apostolate serving? What good was it doing the Maryknoll community? (One of his colleagues denounced to Rome the lecture he gave in Kyoto.) The basic theme of this reaction was obvious: Kennedy had a "deal" going for himself. He didn't have to be a footslogging missionary like the rest of the Maryknollers; he was making money doing something that other missionaries didn't do. This was not a universal reaction, of course, and it certainly wasn't the attitude of the then Maryknoll president who had sent us on our mission to Asia. Furthermore, I dare say that the Maryknoll community is less affected by clerical envy than most other communities and most other dioceses.

In addition to not supporting our own, self-hatred requires that we blind our eyes to the residual anti-Catholic nativism that persists in the country. Only the most naive could believe that the recent Supreme Court decisions on abortion and parochial schools were without anti-Catholic bias. And while I may have some reservations about the strategy of the Respect for Life movement, Marion Sanders's article in *Harper's* on the subject was one of the most vicious, twisted pieces of anti-Catholic writing I have seen in a long time. There was, as far as I am aware, not much outcry against it. The whole "affirmative action" (quota) fad which is sweeping the government and educational institutions is anti-Catholic in fact if not in intent. The distribution of the American population is such that if you discriminate in favor of blacks, you discriminate against Catholics, particularly against Poles and Italians. Some of the Polish and Italian ethnic organizations have complained about this, as has the American Jewish Committee. (In New York, Jews also are the victims of this anti-white discrimination.) But most Catholic leadership, hierarchical and liberal lay, has remained completely silent on the subject. Of all the minority groups in this country Catholics are the least concerned about their own rights and the least conscious of the persistent and systematic discrimination against them in the upper reaches of the corporate and intellectual worlds. When others say that we don't belong there because we are not good enough, we are all too ready to nod our heads in agreement.

The picture is melancholy, self-hating, shallow, pragmatic, anti-intellectual. These are infections in the Catholic body politic which will have to be cured if we are ever to begin to seize the opportunities of the present moment. Imagine, if you will, appearing at a cocktail party of liberal, sophisticated Catholics, lay and clerical, and announcing casually that maybe the most critical problem facing America today is a definition of the nature of original sin and the nature of human nature. You would end up inundated with ice cubes.

What sorts of things ought we to do? (he asked, succumbing ever so slightly to the pragmatic temptation). Clearly there ought to be institutes (I would have called them pastoral institutes if this name hadn't been co-opted to describe marriage markets for the clergy and religious) attached to Catholic universities or affiliated perhaps with non-Catholic universities, in which scholars, wise persons, and idea oriented practitioners could come together to share skills, insights, and resources. There ought to be journals, scholarly and semipopular, devoted to the multidisciplinary examination and interpretation of the American Catholic experience. There ought to be publishing houses producing technical homiletic and catechetic works addressed to the opportunities that challenge us. There ought to be policy-planning commissions, both nationally and locally, to think about the big picture and the long-range future.

Even to list such possibilities is to reveal how sad our present plight is. For no one in his right mind thinks there is the remotest possibility of any of this coming into being for at least the next ten years. The erosion of American Catholicism is almost certain to continue in the short run, and the intellectual and religious opportunities will also be lost in the short run. Individual people, working with creativity and enthusiasm at the grass roots will respond to these opportunities sometimes skillfully, sometimes not. It is perhaps out of their experience that new structures, new styles, new visions will begin to emerge as this century winds down. Until then there is little for us to do but wait and watch sadly as a great institution slowly collapses, the victim not of external enemies but of internal decay.

CHAPTER FOUR

The Triumph
of the Romantics

When he bothers to think about them at all, the communal Catholic knows that those who purport to be the intellectual leaders of the American church are not on his wave length. They dominate the Catholic journals—and therefore he stops subscribing to them; they write the "important" Catholic books—and he does not buy them; they interpret Catholicism to the non-Catholic public—and he wonders if the public is really that gullible. He suspects that most of these "elites" are second-raters who could not have made it in the world outside the church, and take out their anger by attacking the church from within. Above all, he is turned off by their enthusiasm. The communal Catholic is cool, rational, competent. Enthusiastic, undisciplined romantics drive him up the wall.

Yet, they dominate Catholic life today.

For the first five decades of the century, however, American Catholicism was shaped to a considerable extent by the flip side of romanticism, a "fideistic" anti-intellectualism. In other words, the Catholic church had the *answers*. One needed only to look at the teachings of the church, the encyclicals of the popes, the writings of St. Thomas Aquinas to find theoretical and practical solutions for all the major and most of the minor problems of human life. Those who disagreed with us were wrong, so we tried to convert them; and failing at that we had little or nothing to do with them. Too much learning was a dangerous thing; it made for pride and arrogance. Scholars were a luxury at best and troublemakers at worst. The pope, the bishop, the parish priest—these men had the answers, and there was no point in wasting too much time or energy trying to make simple things complicated. If John Courtney Murray was the typical intellectual of the pre-1960 church, so the local parish priest or your favorite novice master or mistress was the typical fideistic anti-intellectual.

In the middle fifties there began a self-conscious attempt, under the auspices of William Rooney and the Catholic Commission on Intellectual and Cultural Affairs, to improve the "climate for respect for learning" in American Catholicism. With the sponsorship of the commission there appeared the famous works by Ellis, Weigel, and O'Day on the American Catholic intellectual life. The publications and the conferences of the commission had an extraordinary impact possibly because the climate was right for them. World War II gave rise to economic expansion and the education benefits of the G.I. Bill that made it possible for American Catholics to catch up with the rest of the American population in educational achievement. Oddly enough, it now seems that by the time the commission's books appeared, lamenting the fact that Catholics were not seeking graduate school training and academic careers in the arts and sciences, the tide had already turned, and Catholics were, if anything, more likely than Protestants to seek such training and pursue professional careers.* Still, the work of the commission and the considerable publicity it received in Catholic journals undoubtedly validated and reinforced the social trends that were already at work. In my research in 1961 on college graduates, for example, I discovered that the brightest students in the Catholic colleges and universities were receiving far

---

*Let me assert that I have no intention of faulting the work of Weigel or Ellis. Both men were dealing with the best data available to them, which were anywhere from five to twenty-five years old. In the middle and late 1950s, there was absolutely no evidence available to suggest that the situation was changing dramatically.

more encouragement from faculty members and advisors to pursue academic careers than were students in other higher educational institutions. Even before Avis, we had discovered that we were number two and had begun to try harder. At the same time, the Cardijn movements were having considerable impact on the lay and clerical elites. These movements vigorously emphasized professional competence and the importance of work and of doing one's work well as a means of witness bearing. A baker was not a baker, for example, in order to provide his bakery as a place for proselytizing; he was a baker to provide bread for people, and he bore witness by providing the best damn bread possible.

Thus, in the rather brief period of time between 1955 and 1965, let us say, there emerged a strong emphasis in American Catholicism on professional competency, academic training, and intellectual skills. It was an exciting era. Ideas were important, competency was critical, skill was decisive. The challenges were immense, the opportunities great even before the euphoria of the Council. And with the intellectual awakening occasioned by the Council, it seemed likely that we would enter a golden age of American Catholic intellectualism. We had the resources, we had the people, we had the ideas, and we even had the European scholars coming here on triumphant lecture tours, collecting immense fees and royalties, who returned to Europe utterly baffled by the apparent hunger of American Catholics for ideas.*

The golden age never came. Indeed, even those who preached competence and scholarship to us a decade and a half ago no longer seem to believe in it, or if they do, they certainly are keeping their mouths shut. American Catholicism did not try intellectualism and find it wanting; it rather found intellectualism hard and decided not to try it. Or, as they say about Texas (unfairly, I think), it proceeded from barbarism to decadence with only a brief stop at civilization.

*My friend Hans Küng remarked to me once, "I'm not a prophet, I am a scholar. Why do American Catholics try to make me into a prophet?" The answer, at least in 1965, would have been, "Hans, they think scholars *are* prophets."

The fideistic anti-intellectualism of the monsignor, the novice master, the seminary rector, and the renaissance monarch archbishop has been replaced by the new anti-intellectualism of the romantic. The new anti-intellectual does not turn to the battered and bedraggled authority of the church for his truth (though he is not above falling back on it and quoting an occasional papal encyclical, as did his predecessors); he rather relies on the authority of feeling, emotion, sensitivity. He would rather feel concern, for example, than be able to define its economic parameters. Analytic self-discipline is rejected out of hand. Mary Daly rejects it on principle. (Theological method, she tells us, is male chauvinism. Ms. Daly probably doesn't realize that from the point of view of the intellectual, she is the chauvinist because she is denying that women are capable of intellectual method.) Daniel Berrigan rejects practicality in principle. ("Everybody worries too much about being practical.") Politics must be the politics of concern and not of compromise and coalition. Fact, evidence, careful dialogue, discussion are a waste of time. Civility is a European or North Atlantic trick designed to keep the third world in subjection. Reality is essentially simple, uncomplicated, and easily known. Something is true if you feel it is true. We are in a crisis, and anything less than a sense of passionate urgency is immoral. Civility, competence, analysis are useless. It is sinful to waste time on such things when there is so much hunger in the world. Of course, if you abandon those things, there is absolutely no risk at all that you might make things worse instead of better.

The most fundamental feeling of the romantic anti-intellectual is the need for self-fulfillment. It may not be a subject that is noticed much in the journals of political and social opinion, but self-fulfillment is the key premise of contemporary Catholic romanticism. The intellectual sees life basically as a search for truth, though he would quickly include goodness and beauty. He would not deny the importance of self-fulfillment, but he would contend that it is something that cannot be sought directly, and also that it can be dangerously deceptive as a norm for behavior. But for the romantic, the quest for personal growth, self-fulfillment, and happiness is the con-

THE TRIUMPH OF THE ROMANTICS

text, the matrix, the unassailable first assumption for all his activity. If a particular commitment or responsibility, enterprise or organization, proves to be unfulfilling then one is automatically dispensed from continuing it. Personal growth, usually defined in the most simplistic categories of pop psychology or the human-potential movement, is the ultimate moral concern, before which all else must yield.

The romantic is also deeply concerned about guilt and self-hatred. The intellectual carefully distinguishes between past situations and present ones, between the injustices of the past and the injustices and mistakes of the present. He is much more concerned about corrective measures against present injustices and the residues of past injustices than he is about assigning responsibility for either the past or the present. He will note, somewhat primly, perhaps, that assigning responsibility doesn't improve the situation. But the romantic feels guilty when there is oppression, misery, or injustice anywhere in the world. He may personally have nothing to do with having caused it, and very likely there is not much he can do to correct it. Still he must confess his guilt, demand admission of guilt from others, and assign collective blame. The ancestors of American Catholics were not here for the most part, during the time of slavery or the conquest of the American Indians. Indeed, they were very likely the victims of similar treatment themselves when they first came to America's shores. Still the romantic demands that we confess our collective guilt and expiate our collective sinfulness. He may be rather short on practical programs, but then he doesn't think they are very important. Once we acknowledge our guilt, expiation can take the form of giving up what we have to those who don't. (This delights the recipients, of course—although their resentment is often so strong they will continue to resent us for the giving as much as for the having—a no-win situation for us.) The world will then be a better place.

The romantic is preoccupied with collectivities. The intellectual is a universalist; he believes in abstract principles, frequently meritocratic in form. A man is judged by who he is and what he can do personally. But the romantic's feelings tell him that mystical bonds tie groups of people together. Therefore, collective guilt and collective innocence, collective classes which oppress and collective classes which are oppressed, exist in the world; hence, some collectivities are good and some are not. Blacks, young people, women, the third world are good groups; whites, older people, men, Western Europe, and especially Americans are bad. Even though any given male Italian-American may never have personally done anything to oppress a black or a woman, he must still yield his promotion to a black or to a woman to compensate for the bad things that white males have done to blacks and women in the past. It will do him no good, incidentally, to argue that in his tradition women are treated much better than they are in the Anglo-Saxon American tradition, and that neither he nor his ancestors ever oppressed any black. The romantic has decided that he is part of the oppressor class, and he must pay for being a part of that class whatever his personal innocence may be.

The romantic believes that it is essential to identify with the victim. The intellectual argues that you cannot identify with someone very different from yourself without the risk of alienation and self-destruction. To sympathize and empathize with the victim, to do everything in your power to free him from his victimization is possible, but you cannot *become* the victim. These distinctions are unacceptable for the romantic. He does not feel right unless he sides with the victim against his own oppressing class. Of course, siding with him does not mean living with him or taking on his life-style—God forbid. It means rather to debase oneself in his presence (or those members of the victim's group who happen to hold Ph.D.'s) and support his cause in conversation. To identify with the victim usually means to take his side in an argument rather than to support policies that might really ameliorate his situation or which the majority of his group supports (which usually turns out to be what everyone else supports, too). You see, most of the victim class are victims of false consciousness, so to identify properly with the victim, one must identity with the vanguard of the victim class, that is to say, with those victims whose consciousnesses have been raised, who usually turn out to be those victims with graduate school training or those who have learned to repeat ideologically correct words and phrases.

The romantic, then, is preoccupied with false consciousness and consciousness raising as an issue rather than as a personal activity (his consciousness has been raised, of course). The intellectual, like Peter Berger, will insist on "cognitive participation" and "cognitive respect." He will wonder about the arrogance of those who pretend to know a whole group's needs better than its members know it. He will be concerned, as one deviant woman theologian remarked to me, about the possibility that the 99 percent of American women who stand between the "total woman" and Mary Daly may possibly have a contribution to make in the discussion of women's rights. But the romantic could not care less about the statistical majority. He feels that he is a member of the vanguard group, and the vanguard has a missionary role to preach to and to convert those who do not understand how they are being victimized, those Paulo Freire says are little better than horses. There is, of course, nothing to learn from such people, no need to respect them or the possibility that they may have useful insights. They may pretend to respect them while preparing the next phase of the argument or the peroration of the rhetoric, but it is a tactic not a belief. Usually the urgency of the situation is such that pretense must be abandoned. Consciousness raising is almost necessarily a crash course.

Confrontation is the favorite tactic of the romantic anti-intellectual. The intellectual wants to know about goals, the appropriateness of means to achieve the goals, the most effective strategy, the best way to win allies, and a whole host of other detailed political questions that presume careful and cautious analysis of the situation. The outrage, the concern, the passion, the guilt of the romantic precludes the raising of such questions. How could anyone expect the Berrigans and their allies to ask whether their tactics were counterproductive, or whether they were alienating potential allies? People were dying in Vietnam; there was no time to worry about tactics. We must "confront America," David O'Brien tells us in the first essay in the bishops' bicentennial discussion guide. The intellectual may wonder how the hell you confront America. Do you throw a picket line around all the borders of the republic? What does confronting America mean operationally in terms of personnel, organization, strategy, tactics? When you ask that question, the romantic anti-intellectual looks at you pityingly and simply repeats that America is an immoral society and *must* be confronted.

For the romantic, experience is of primary importance. Priests don't know anything about marriage, people over thirty cannot speak truly about the problems of the younger generation, you can't discuss Pentecostalism unless you have participated in one of their sessions, you can't understand what it is like to be oppressed unless you have been oppressed, no man can hope to speak to the religious problems of women, and no European theologian can say anything at all that could concern the third world—although, of course, Europeans should listen to what the third world has to say. If you haven't experienced it, in other words, keep your mouth shut, unless you happen to be a member of one of the groups on the schedule of "approved" oppressed. The intellectual would argue that you can discuss a subject without having experienced it if you have sensitivity, empathy, insight, and have pursued the relevant literature. The intellectual would contend that some men could write novels about women that were better than many women could write, and the converse is true, of course. Some white scholars, like Timothy Smith and Eugene Genovese, can write very effectively about black religion.*

*I once heard two very angry blacks at a session of the American Historical Association try to tear apart Timothy Smith for an absolutely brilliant paper on black religion (showing, incidentally, it was not a rationalization of the acceptance of oppression and slavery). They could not refute Smith's data or analysis because he knew far more about the subject than they did; his research was overwhelmingly persuasive. Their principal argument was simply that a white man should not dare to say anything about black religion, much less that black religion kept human dignity and human longing for freedom alive under the most difficult possible circumstances. Smith, a polite and charming man, took it all very calmly, although he told me afterward that the article had been rejected by a number of historical reviews on the very grounds that it was an inappropriate subject for a white historian.

The romantic anti-intellectual delights in dissecting the motives of his adversaries. The intellectual eschews this mode of analysis on principle; he tries to keep to the substance of the discussion—a principle honored in the breach often enough. But the romantic delights in psychohistory, because it enables him to explain the "resistance" of his adversaries to the truth which the romantic possesses. "La Furiosa," Rosemary Ruether, periodically sends forth vicious psychoanalyses of those who dare to disagree with her. She does not have access, of course, to their psychological records, if any, but true romantic that she is, she needs no evidence; she feels the emotional problems of those who are wrong. Hence she has little trouble describing their psyches in great detail.

Even though he repeatedly confesses his guilt, the romantic is strongly convinced of his own morality and virtue. The intellectual considers morality to be a gray and uncertain matter. For him there are few clear cut moral choices. When someone tells him that particular solutions are the moral ones, he doesn't quite know what to make of the argument, for he can think of several arguments in favor of the morality of the opposite solution. The romantic, filled with a sense of urgency and concern and enthusiasm to do something about injustice, has no patience with such casuistic quibbling. The world is filled with clear cut moral choices. Instead of discussing morality, we ought to be *doing* the moral thing. The romantic feels so powerfully, so strongly about the morality and virtue of the cause he has embraced, anyone who wants to discuss it with him must necessarily be unconcerned, conservative, or, quite possibly, a hardened cynic to entertain the thought that there might be an alternative position.

The romantic believes in fresh new starts. That is why he is so enthusiastic about young people. The intellectual doubts the possibility of new starts, arguing that we are all shaped by our own heritages and cannot cast them off. He also thinks it is possible to learn from one's heritage. He does not believe the present generation is the hinge of history, and he wonders if young people are really all that different from their parents. But the romantic has little respect for the past and not much more for the present. As Margaret Mead says, approving of the young people about whom she fantasizes in *Culture and Commitment*, the romantic has his feet solidly planted in the future. The only kind of past which he is interested in talking about is his personal past, his autobiography, which he will repeat endlessly if given the chance. The romantic theology, to the extent that it exists at all, is little more than religious autobiography. The romantic communicates intellectually with others by telling them his story, listening somewhat impatiently while they tell him theirs, and then plunging on ahead with more of his own.

Romantics are prone to join movements. The intellectual is cautious about collective behavior. He is skeptical of the effervescence (to use Durkheim's word) which characterizes social movements, of their undirected enthusiasm, and of the authoritarian control they can impose on their members. But the romantic delights in the enthusiasm of an effervescent movement, and welcomes its authoritarian control. The Berrigan anti-war movement may have been rigid and autocratic, but the point, you see, was that since the Berrigans were against the war, how could anyone possibly disagree with them? How could one fail to be swept along by the moral excellence of their vision and by the enthusiasm of their personal witness and commitment?

If John Murray was the quintessential intellectual, and if the novice master of your choice was the quintessential fideist anti-intellectual, then Daniel Berrigan, with his passion, his enthusiasm, his intensity, and his virtue, was the quintessential romantic anti-intellectual. When the young Jesuits from the Center for Concern looked for a model, they could have chosen either Murray or Berrigan. That they unhesitantly and unquestionably accepted Berrigan is as good a summary as any, I think, of the triumph of the romantics. They have carried the day completely. There is no longer any effective opposition to them. One need only look at *Liberty and Justice for All,* the official discussion guide for American Catholic celebration of the bicentennial, to see how complete their victory·has been.

The romantic anti-intellectualism of the last decade has given power and drive to the various movements which have swept through the church. First of all, we had the religious education movement, which promised that if we used up to date (read "European academic") techniques of religious instruction, we could do away with the need for Catholic schools and produce a whole new generation of deeply committed, socially alert Catholics. Oddly enough, they produced instead the highest apostasy rate in history. Then the Cursillo arrived on the scene, which promised that by using slightly modified Spanish fascist indoctrination techniques, we could produce instant Christians after a weekend of intensive brainwashing. The sensitivity-encounter craze came next, and a vast number of priests and religious set themselves up as instant psychotherapists. This put a fair number of them and their patients in the hospital before many finally ended up marrying each other. Then the Berrigan radicals thought you could end the war by pouring blood on draft records, and the feminist movement turned loose on the church a horde of castrating nuns, who now had ideological justification for expressing the hatred of men they had always felt. Next came the charismatics, babbling incoherently and justifying a return to the most primitive kind of religious and ascetical fundamentalism. Then the reconciliation-bicentennial-third world craze came along, which argued that Americans could expiate their guilt by matching the Latin American theology of liberation with a North American "theology of relinquishment." Now we have the Right to Life movement, which manages to synthesize marvelously the old and the new anti-intellectualism, the old fideism with the new romanticism. In the midst of all this there is also an ethnic movement. Here people can celebrate their warm and good feelings about ethnics (read "the ordinary American Catholic who picks up the bill for the other movements"). Whether the ethnics feel good about any movement which proclaims them to be victims is a question to which there is no satisfactory answer as yet.

I am dyspeptic on the subject of movements. Movement enthusiasm and party line, it seems to me, are only a substitute for thought, and, as an unreconstructed intellectual, I am for thought, not its counterfeit. I am fully prepared to admit that there are more than a few grains of truth in all the movements I have just described. They all have something important to say, but unfortunately, like Chesterton heretics they have a grip on a part of the truth and think it is the whole.

In any event, the movement does not require qualified, nuanced acceptance of some propositions; a movement demands faith. Movements must have their folk heroes, because people are far more important than ideas. Rahner and Schillebeeckx were quoted not so long ago with the same passionate devotion that was reserved for Thomas Aquinas in the 1950s (and with the same comprehension that Aquinas enjoyed). The Berrigan brothers, folk heroes par excellence, are now somewhat tarnished, but still adored by their admirers (Philip Berrigan, we were told in *The New Yorker,* is the kind of person who makes you feel like falling down and begging for absolution). Paulo Freire and Gustavo Gutierez are the current fashionable demigods of the Year of Reconciliation-bicentennial-third world craze. (And God help you if you say anything against them.) It would appear that Richard Barnett is on the way to becoming a folk hero in Catholic circles because of his book on the multinational corporations. The point about folk heroes is that it is forbidden to discuss or analyze their ideas. They are sacred personages and must be reverenced and respected as such. It is almost blasphemous to want to submit their assertions to the profane scrutiny of intellectual analysis. They are great and sincere men, they are concerned, they are involved, they care. How dare some dry, dull academic come along and raise questions about the accuracy of their assertions.

The movements are anti-American for the most part. American Catholics have never felt very confident of their own resources and have always looked abroad for guidance—the faculties of the Roman seminary first, then the French worker-priests in urban missionaries, then the German and Dutch theologians, and now, heaven save us, the Latin American theologians, who have virtually no influence in their own countries. Perhaps the classic example of the anti-American strain in the movements is the enthusiasm with which the religious education movement sent its young people to study in European catechetical centers, such as *Lumen Vitae*. Here were to be found modern and progressive techniques of religious education. In fact, the pedagogical methods taught at these centers were the same techniques being used in the educational psychology departments of a dozen American Catholic universities fifteen or twenty years ago. David O'Brien's introduction to the bicentennial discussion guide of the bishops contains almost nothing about the American political and social heritage, not a word about Madison and Hamilton, a passing reference to Thomas Jefferson, nothing about Lincoln. The American heritage is worthless, apparently, for even stirring up social consciousness in response to its ideals.

The movement types are particularly nasty in writing off last year's heroes. Garry Wills, a sometime Jesuit scholastic, who singlehandedly, it seemed, with an article in *Playboy*, was able to get Woodstock Seminary closed down, destroyed former folk heroes Jacqueline Grennan and John Courtney Murray in vicious and unfair chapters in his *Bare Ruined Choirs*. Former Sister Grennan is able to defend herself, but as far as I know, none of Murray's Jesuit colleagues or his other great friends and admirers rose up to defend that American Catholic giant against the vicious charge of being "the theologian of the Cold War." Fashions change among movements, and as you move from one to another (and there are quite a few priests, religious, and elite lay folk who have made it for a time in all the movements described here), you have to be very agile about abandoning former positions and earlier favorites.

Turning against former heroes is partly the result of the powerful strain of resentment that is characteristic of the movements. I am endlessly surprised at the capacity of many romantics to really hate the people who have been erected as their enemies. At one meeting of the Catholic Committee on Urban Ministry at Notre Dame, several of the participants discussed how ashamed they were of the Catholic laity. The ordinary Catholic, according to Monsignor Charles Owen Rice, was a racist, a bigot, and a hawk; Rice was terribly embarrassed to belong to the same church they do.* Similarly, an American theologian of quite limited talent confessed to me at the Brussels *Concilium* Congress that she and a number of other people who should never have been let in were making life miserable for Hans Küng and Edward Schillebeeckx. "You've got to understand, Andrew, that ordinary people like me rarely get a chance to cut someone like Küng down to our own size." In his book, *Envy,* the German sociologist and philosopher Helmut Schoeck suggests that envy is one of the factors at work in every social movement. It would be a mistake to underestimate the importance of envy (if disguised) in the romantic movement of American Catholicism. Secretly, many of the romantics wish they were intellectuals, or at least they wish they had the intellectual's command of fact and language. It becomes necessary to cut them down to size.

For a romantic anti-intellectual, there is only one side to an argument: the right one, the one he *feels* is right. The Catholic Committee on Urban Ministry, for example, will bring economist Richard Barnett to Notre Dame to suggest that the American economic system does not work. It will not, however, bring George Stigler or Milton Friedman to present the opposite case. (These two latter worthies are not among my favorite people, but they would annihilate Barnett and just about anyone else, too.) Peter Henriot presents one version of American international responsibility in the bicentennial discussion guide, but one hears nothing from Daniel P. Moynihan. The National Conference of Catholic Bishops' Committee on Human Development issues a booklet on income redistribution in which all the redistributionist arguments are presented with no counterarguments from the other side. One hears nothing of Irving Kristol or of James Coleman's devastating review of Christopher Jencks' *Inequality.* In none

---

*Faced with data that suggested he might have been harsh in his judgment, Monsignor Rice did not retreat—another case of "you and your damn data!"

of the discussions of the peace movement is there any reference to the work of Howard Schuman or James Wright, which seems to confirm beyond any reasonable doubt that the movement was mostly counterproductive. Nor in discussions of the third world are there references to the books by Donald Eugene Smith about religion and economic development. Nor have I noted any reference to Bernard Weinraub's superb reporting on India or Penny Lernoux's on Venezuela with their discussions of the specific structural and cultural problems of individual third world countries. Such discussions are not worth the effort, apparently, because the problems of the third world countries are entirely caused by the United States. One therefore need not distinguish among these countries and analyze the problems of each one carefully, since there is only one problem: the imperialism of the American government and the multinational corporations.

How did it all happen? How did the "climate of respect for learning" turn into "concern"? The whole American cultural elite went through an orgy of romantic anti-intellectualism in the 1960s, and Catholics, with their remarkable ability to discover a new cultural style last, began to imitate the anti-intellectualism of the mainstream precisely when those elites were having second thoughts about it. Similarly, the universal church has also turned away from rationality after the splendid theological achievements of the Vatican Countil. *Humanae Vitae* was a classic anti-intellectual exercise. The pope listed the arguments for a change in the birth control position, but then did not even bother to respond to them. He simply insisted that the prohibition of birth control was a teaching of Jesus Christ (apparently assuming that if he said it was a part of the teaching of Jesus, Catholics would take his word for it). Cardinal Koenig showed up at the University of Chicago (as part of a gimmick for its desperate fund raising drive) and embarrassed the Catholics in the audience (but delighted the Cardinal Archbishop of Chicago) by a crude and gratuitous attack on sociology. The international journal *Concilium* turned its attention to almost everything but theology, and most recently it has moved toward discussions of international economic problems without any benefit of the expertise which might be obtained by trained economic advisors on its staff. Freire and Gutierez terrorized the editorial board of *Concilium* and forced these "European" theologians to debase themselves before the superior third world morality. Indeed, one issue was taken away from its normal editors and a different topic imposed on them by Freire and Gutierez. The humiliation of the editors was justified on the grounds that one of them had worked for the West German government.

And while the Council was a monumental intellectual achievement, the disillusionment that came after it made many people wonder how important complex theological ideas were after all. They were not strong enough to resist the curial reactions or to inhibit the disastrous appointments made by Archbishops Vanozzi and Raimund when they were apostolic delegates. (The appointments of successors to Cardinals Ritter of St. Louis and Meyer of Chicago may easily have been the two worst appointments in the history of American Catholicism.) Nor did rational arguments prevent the disaster of *Humanae Vitae,* which our research has now demonstrated to be the principal cause of the decline in American Catholicism. (It was not the Council.)

The curial reaction, the postconciliar appointments of archbishops (until the arrival of Archbishop Jadot), and *Humanae Vitae* helped to create a climate of anti-intellectualism in the American church similar to that produced in the rest of American society by war, race riots, and assassinations.

Many of the clergy and religious, and some of the elite laity in the middle years of life, experienced acute personality disorganizations in the years after the Council. The organizational and theological structures of apologetic Catholicism seemed to collapse overnight. These men and women had never really been faced with the challenge of faith before; they now found they had to make fundamental religious choices not in their early twenties, when most people make such choices, but in their middle years. At the same time, respect for the Catholic tradition seemed to vanish. Even in the attenuated form with which this tradition was presented by apologetic Catholicism, it had some rationality to it. Thomas Aquinas, Newman, Chesterton, for example, were swept out with the bath water. Chesterton, it was hinted, was anti-Semitic, Thomas Aquinas was dismissed as irrelevant, and no one ever reads Newman any more. Catholic tradition was either ridiculed by such books as *The Last Catholic in America* or covered with superficial nostalgia by writers like Garry Wills. In either case, there was no support or substance to be gained from reading them. Finally, many clergy and religious were only half-educated. A course or two here, a semester off there, a couple of books read, some weekend experiences, and one was ready to set up as a do-it-yourself prophet or expert. Surveys were designed overnight, religious communities were drastically reformed in a week of meetings, policy statements were put together in a weekend by a committee, and discussion guides were put together haphazardly by busy and overworked staffs. Everybody was being sincere and honest and open and concerned and working terribly hard. Who needed any more education?

One must also give considerable weight to the *traison de clercs,* the betrayal of rationality by the Catholic cultural elites. As official interpreters of American Catholicism to the rest of the world, Wilfrid Sheed and Garry Wills replaced thought with cleverness and sometimes, preciousness. This appeals to the prejudices of those who consume their writing, but it hardly makes for understanding. Thus Sheed can say that Catholicism requires a culture but there is no culture in America, hence American Catholicism is in trouble. This clever and superficial line appeals to the readers of *The New York Review of Books* who are delighted that there is no culture in the United States (save for their own, of course). And Garry Wills can provide a rich description of his own voyage from conservative classicism to Berriganism and persuade his readers that his story is *the* story of American Catholicism. It is great fun and very well written, but that kind of Catholic chic is hardly a substitute for disciplined research and analysis. And those lay and clerical leaders who spoke, not so much to the world outside the church but to the church itself, have pretty much remained silent in the face of the romantics. Daniel Callahan, Peter Steinfels, the younger Michael Novak, George Higgins, and John Egan challenged neither the Berrigans nor their romantic successors. An occasional intellectual like Edward Duff even went over to the enemy. Some of the cultural elites saw no problem with the Berrigan movement, others would confess privately and off the record that they disagreed with the means but approved the ends— forgetting what they said fifteen years previously to the supporters of Joe McCarthy who used exactly the same line. Nor has a single one of the "old Catholic Action" voices been raised against the incompetencies and the simplicities of *Liberty and Justice for All*.

The bishops have played a curious role in the triumph of romanticism. As far as I am aware, not one episcopal voice was ever raised against the abuses of the Cursillo or the sensitivity-encounter crazes; and the charismatic movement certainly has their discreet toleration if not support. Furthermore, they have put the seal of official approval on liberation theology with their bicentennial discussion guide. Fifteen years ago one would not have anticipated that the bishops would have yielded so easily to fashion. The key, I think, is the uneasiness most bishops feel in the presence of an intellectual or scholar.* The hierarchy is relatively modest in the scholarly achievements of its members. There is nothing wrong with that. But many bishops still have, at least semi-consciously, the image of a bishop as an answer-giver, the one who knows the answers to all questions on every subject. Thus, a bishop is very uneasy when he is in the presence of a scholar like Raymond Brown, who clearly knows far more about St. John than the bishop can ever hope to. Brown is

*Lest any bishop who should happen to know my phone number call me at 2:30 in the morning, let me be very precise: there are some bishops who have a great respect for learning, for intelligence, for disciplined rationality, and professional competence. They are as sickened by the romantic triumph as I am—and often much more colorful in their language on the subject. In this chapter I am speaking about a climate which permeates the hierarchy, not about every bishop. I think it's fair to say, though, that my description is accurate for a substantial number of them.

perceived as a threat to the bishop's role as teacher. The charismatics, as well as the people from the Center for Concern, do not threaten the bishops intellectually, and they are for the most part quite pious and sincere. Intellectual competency is not something avidly sought by the American hierarchy; indeed it is often not tolerated.

In addition, some of the bishops must feel considerable guilt for the disasters that have fallen on the church. They must have some sense that their two-faced attitude on *Humanae Vitae* (supporting it in public but winking at clerical advice against it in private) contributed substantially to the deterioration of the credibility of the church for the average lay person. Someone like Cardinal Dearden, for example, who delivered the bicentennial celebration into the hands of the romantic leftists, has a good deal to feel guilty about. He presided over the American church during one of the most spectacular collapses in the whole history of Catholicism. He did little, as far as one can tell, to counter the deterioration. The report on the American church, presented to the Synod of Bishops last year in Rome (prepared by an official of the public relations staff—he's no threat!) and approved by Dearden, seems to suggest that the reason for the deterioration of American Catholicism is the materialism of American Catholics. It is but a short step from that to the blatant anti-Americanism of *Liberty and Justice for All*.

There is, then, less intellectualism in the ecclesial Catholic community now than there was when O'Day, Ellis, and Weigel wrote their books in the 1950s. The communal Catholics, of course, continue to be intellectual, but their concerns are focused away from the church. Paradoxically, the communal Catholics are in the same position as the ordinary Catholic laity. Both discount the church's credibility as a social teacher, and neither will take seriously the indoctrination and consciousness raising which the official church, dominated by the romantics, is engaging in. As Professor Pastora San Juan Cafferty commented to me apropo of *Liberty and Justice for All*, "Thank heaven my people don't go to church or join discussion groups. They won't have to put up with that foolishness."

It is practically impossible for the communal Catholic to work with the romantic-dominated institutional church. He is urged to reconciliation, but the price for it is to admit that the passionate feeling of romanticism is at least as valid toward the solution of social and political problems as disciplined thought. If a communal Catholic intellectual is told, in effect, that piety and concern make the second-rate first-rate and the mediocre excellent, he simply cannot agree. He does not believe it is true. He may not dislike those who think it is true, but reconciliation or collaboration with them is impossible in principle. As Jaroslav Pelikan remarked so long ago, "There is no 'logue' for the dialogue." In fact, from the point of view of the romantic anti-intellectuals, "logue" is not important anyhow.

Paradoxically, romanticism's supreme triumph comes just at the time when American Catholic theology (however unread it is) is beginning to move into a golden era of creativity. On the basis of my dealings with the best of the European theologians on *Concilium,* I can say unequivocally that the American Catholic theological era has begun. (In complete contrast to the rest of the workbook, David Tracy's brief discussion of the church in *Liberty and Justice for All* is a first-rate exercise in intellectualism.) Indeed, the convergence of styles of thought about religion in anthropology, sociology, psychology, literary criticism, exegesis, history, and philosophy is one of the most remarkable phenomena of our time. Out of this convergence is emerging the raw material for an extraordinarily effective new catechetic and homiletic for an approach to religion grounded in human experience, as any meaningful approach to religion must be. To grasp the implication of this theological and scholarly revolution and to develop those catechetic and homiletic tools they imply will require deep thought and disciplined effort. But I'm afraid this is not the time for that sort of thing, and it's not likely to be for many years to come.

The American Catholic ecclesial community is still caught in the 1960s. Anti-intellectual romanticism is moribund in the rest of the country. It was sustained for a time by Watergate and is now barely alive because of the current economic problems of the country. But when the economy improves it is almost certain that there will be a resurgence of serious scholarly study of the American experience spurred by the bicentennial year. There will be a new blossoming of intellectualism and professionalism in many areas of national life. The Overseas Development Council (presided over by Theodore Hesburgh—certainly no romantic) is light years ahead of the church in the sophistication of its approach to both the problems of international economics and in its understanding of the dynamics of American public opinion. This is but one example of the kinds of things that could be done with the institutional encouragement, recognition, or even support of the church, but Catholicism is still like Avis, number two. Despite all our efforts in the last twenty years, as an organization we seem to have fallen even further behind.

Catholicism will persist. It always has and the evidence suggests that it always will. Faith is not based on either the virtue or the intelligence of church elites. The Bridegroom is not to be judged by the spouse; she will be without blemish only when He returns. But in our current American Catholic manifestation, she has one hell of a case of acne.

CHAPTER FIVE

The Return of the Nativist

If the romantics drive the communal Catholic up the wall, he is horrified to discover the persistence of vigorous and bigoted anti-Catholic nativism in American life. Like everyone else, he thought nativism died in 1960, when the first Catholic president was elected, but when *The New York Times Magazine* (in an article by Richard Reeves) assures its readers that Jesuits teach that the end justifies the means, the communal Catholic is badly shaken. Just as he can no longer expect intellectual leadership from his church, so now, he finds he can no longer expect an open mind from all of his non-Catholic colleagues.

Father Theodore Hesburgh, president of the University of Notre Dame, is one of the "good guys," a certified, card-carrying "unknockable." Vigorous supporter of civil rights, strong advocate of amnesty, outspoken critic of the Pope and the President, Hesburgh's credentials are impeccable. So when he warns Americans of a possible surge in Catholic anger, he must be taken seriously:

Lately, I have perceived some stirrings among these quiet, faithful, patriotic, modest American Catholics. They are beginning to feel set upon, ignored, even badly used and unappreciated. Let me illustrate from the past year's happenings. Last year, fifty million American

Catholics wanted two things, first, some help—even modest—to the parochial schools that educated many of their children as they desired, and secondly, no liberalization of the laws on abortion. What happened? The Catholics were denied help to parochial schools and abortion was made legal practically on demand for any reason. Even I am upset when my own brother says he could get a tax credit if he paid for an abortion, but not for the considerable expense he pays for his children's attendance at three different Catholic schools.*

In other words, what has already happened in New York may well be happening nationally. Presumably the bafflement of New York liberals (mostly Jewish) will spread to their national counterparts. Why can't you win an election with four Jews and a black on the ticket? Why won't Catholics vote for their moral, intellectual, and political betters? Why did Catholics from Queens, Nassau, and Suffolk counties, who voted so enthusiastically for Robert Kennedy, vote for James Buckley? Why did Catholics defect from the Democratic party for the first time in history to vote against Senator McGovern? (It should be noted, however, that Catholics defected no more than other Democrats.) What's the matter with Catholics anyway? Why aren't they the good, loyal Democrats they are supposed to be?

The answer is that Catholics have left the Democratic party because they were thrown out. If, as Father Hesburgh suggests, there is a growing Catholic restiveness in the country, the reason is Catholics are slowly becoming aware that nativism is alive and well in the United States. If one quarter of the American population feels left out the reason is they have been. In the Midwest we still run Catholics for public office, and Catholics still vote Democratic. But then the Midwest is a backward, conservative part of the country—where liberal Democrats like Humphrey, Mondale, Hartke, Bayh, Stevenson, Nelson, Proxmire, Hart, etc., etc., have been known to win elections.

Is nativism alive and well in the country? You'd better believe it.

*Address given by the Rev. Theodore M. Hesburgh at the National Convention of the Catholic Press Association, April 24, 1974, Denver, Colorado, pp. 19–20.

ITEM: The stereotypical white ethnic—meaning racist, hard hat, ignorant, hawk, slob—is a euphemism for Catholic. You can denounce white ethnics and still feel virtuous that you are not anti-Catholic, even though all white ethnics seem to be Catholic. And of course you need not be deterred by the data that show ethnic Catholics are less likely to be racist and more likely to have been against the Vietnam war from the beginning. You can also ignore the fact that for forty years the ethnics have supported every major liberal economic and social reform that has come down the turnpike, and their elected representatives have voted for such measures. Catholics are conservative and that is that.

ITEM: A number of different data sets show that while anti-black and anti-Jewish feelings among Catholics have been declining, anti-Catholic feeling among blacks and Jews has been increasing. Apparently you need a scapegoat for the problems of American society. You can't blame Jews or blacks because racism and anti-Semitism are unfashionable; so you blame Catholics because nativism has never really been acknowledged and is much less unfashionable. These data have been in the possession of several Jewish agencies for some time, but I am unaware of any concern about it.

ITEM: The Institute of Urban Life in Chicago finds that Poles and Italians are almost totally absent from the boards of large corporations. The various keepers of the nation's conscience, like the National Council of Churches, would have worked themselves into paroxysms of guilt if the finding concerned blacks; yet they remained completely silent.

ITEM: One hears it said and nauseam that the white ethnics have "made it" in American society and blacks and other nonwhite groups have not. But when elaborate demographic data are prepared to refute this claim, Professor Nam, the editor of *Demography,* ships the data back with a reviewer's comment that no one would be interested in it. (Incidentally, how you can have made it and still be a blue collar ethnic is an inconsistency that does not disturb the neonativist.)

ITEM: Catholics are invisible on the senior faculties of great universities. When one asks why, one is told that blacks and women are absent because of discrimination, Catholics because of intellectual inferiority. (I was told at one university that if I left the priesthood then an appointment could be arranged.)

ITEM: Catholics are just about nonexistent on the boards and staffs of large foundations. And the token Catholics who are present on a few are constantly harassed by overtly nativist memos (one which spoke anxiously that the doors of the foundation were darkened by Catholic priests).

ITEM: Other groups can pursue their goals in American society with impunity. When Catholics do so it becomes part of a plot of the hierarchy—never mind that the hierarchy in its present state couldn't lead a pack of starved vampires to a blood bank.

ITEM: The United States is the only country in the western hemisphere which does not aid parochial schools. Men are appointed to the Supreme Court whose anti-Catholic feelings are well known. If a justice had refused to attend the wedding of his daughter to a black or Jew, can you imagine his appointment being confirmed? Under such circumstances Catholics may be excused for being skeptical of the shoddy legal arguments of the "entanglement" doctrine.

ITEM: The official interpreters of American Catholicism in the national media are all individuals who have departed in one way or another from the mainline Catholic community (Garry Wills, Wilfrid Sheed, Michael Harrington, Robert Sam Anson, Pete Hamill, etc.). The argument in response is that you can't be an intelligent person and remain a practicing Catholic, but Anson's sloppy article in *New Times* on Irish power in the church (ignoring the fact that Boston's bishop is Portuguese, Brooklyn's and Cincinnati's are Italian, and Philadelphia's is Polish) would hardly have been printed if it were about blacks or Jews. And can you imagine *New York* magazine using Hamill's proud boast that the "new Irish" (whoever the hell they are) think like Jews, if such self-hatred came from a black? Or can you imagine what would happen if Polish jokes were told about Chicanos?

ITEM: The anti-abortion issue, led by four pathetic cardinals presenting their views before Congress, is described as a Catholic plot to impose its moral views on society. In fact, the hierarchy jumped on the anti-abortion bandwagon only when they discovered belatedly (as always) that they had a mass movement on their hands that could easily get out of control. As evidence of the plot, everyone cites the National Opinion Research Center's (NORC) finding that Catholics, as well as Protestants, are in favor of abortion. (*The New Republic* somehow managed to confuse NORC with Gallup, however, thereby revealing how careful their editorial research was.) Actually, what the NORC article showed (and I ought to know since I wrote it) was that while the overwhelming majority of Catholics and Protestants support abortion if the mother's life is in danger or there is a risk of delivering a defective child, the majority of both groups are against abortion if the woman simply does not want any more children. Thus, by opposing abortion on demand, the Catholic hierarchy is speaking for the conscience of the American majority—however crude and inept it may be as a spokesman. Don't hold your breath to read that in *The New York Times*.

ITEM: A Jewish leader chided me because Catholics were not vigorous enough in their support of Israel. It was not, he told me, high enough on our agenda. I asked him how high Ulster was on his. He told me that was different. How different? Well, the killing in Ulster was senseless violence, and the Irish had never been the victims of genocide. I asked him if he had ever heard of Cromwell, and he asked me what that had to do with it.

ITEM: In her nasty response to those who had the temerity to criticize her anti-abortion plot article in *Harper's,* Marion Sanders says that from the grammar and syntax of her critics it is clear that the writers are not regular readers of *Harper's.* How can you possibly have a dialogue with semi-literate Catholics? And Hunter Thompson, in his freaked-out account of the McGovern loss (he lost because he wasn't radical enough) throws the word "Catholic" into his litany of unpleasant adjectives about Thomas Eagleton. Ms. Sanders and Dr. Thompson nativists? But they're such nice people. I know some racists who are nice people, too.

ITEM: In the grand purification of the Democratic party in 1972, designed by Professor Galbraith and executed by Senator McGovern's wunderkinder, it was the Catholics who got thrown out to make way for the black, young, brown, and female. The old party stalwarts were called "big city bosses" and "labor czars"; that they were also Catholic was "just the way things worked out."

ITEM: *The New York Times* editorializes that ethnic politics is "an immigrant-born virus." The editorial writer refuses to believe, in a time as sophisticated as ours, people worry very much about the religious composition of a political ticket. It is not the "new minorities" the writer has in mind; he makes that quite clear. And it surely isn't the Jews because the issue was a Democratic ticket that was entirely Jewish. So the immigrants that brought the virus are the Catholic immigrants, and Catholic style politics is an infection which one simply cannot tolerate in a civilized society (and never mind that group politics originated with James Madison not with Catholic immigrants (see the tenth and fifty-first Federalist Papers).

ITEM: Richard Reeves, in *New York* magazine, celebrating the demise of Richard Nixon, is astonished. Who would believe that a political hack like Peter Rodino could have been instrumental in the downfall of Nixon? Were he from New York instead of Jersey, Mr. Rodino would have long since been replaced by a reform congressman.

ITEM: *Science,* one of the most prestigious scholarly journals in the nation, publishes an article by a psychologist purporting to show that Catholicism is the most antithetical to scholarship of all the denominations in the United States. The researcher uses data that are fifteen years old, engages in fallacies and argumentation that would get him a failing grade in any introductory methodology course, generalizes outrageously about Catholicism, and ignores a substantial body of careful empirical research published over the last ten years in the *American Journal of Sociology,* which used much better data and showed just the opposite. Yet when the editor of *Science* is asked to apologize for the affront to Catholicism, he bluntly refuses to do so.

ITEM: The *Christian Century,* in an editorial comment on the Edelin abortion trial, noted that the trial had taken place in *South* Boston which had recently been disgraced by the busing controversy. The victims, observed the writer, had now victimized with a vengeance. In fact, the trial had taken place in the Suffolk County Courthouse which is not in *South* Boston but near Beacon Hill; and the jury was not selected from *South* Boston but from the entire city of Boston (plus Revere and Chelsea). One geographical adjective served to subtly but effectively link two unconnected events—unconnected that is save in the new anti-Catholicism of the angry liberal Protestant mind. There was no evidence in the editorial that any of the jurors came from *South* Boston nor that any of them were for or against busing. The link was completely gratuitous but it served admirably to reinforce the prejudices of the liberal Protestant sensibility: Catholics cannot be trusted to give a fair trial to a black doctor accused of abortion. Strangely the *Christian Century* never once raised the question of whether black jurors in Washington could be trusted to give a fair trial to the Nixon-Watergate crowd.

ITEM: Historian Martin Marty of the University of Chicago writes apropos of the Selma anniversary, "The new populist and ethnic machismo teaches us to say that the whites of Selma were all right; never try to change anyone—including yourself. Protect your tribal interests." None of the Catholics who have written about ethnicity (some who like Paul Asciola were at Selma, by the way) have ever written anything of the sort, as Dean Marty must know. They have argued that you must try to understand other people's problems from the inside. They have insisted that sweeping judgments about broad categories of people—like "The Whites of Selma"—are unjustified.

In any case, as the tenth anniversary reports on Selma indicated, the people of that city *had* changed. There are blacks on the town council, the police force, and the high school basketball team. Indeed, blacks are far more adequately represented in Selma than Catholics are on the senior faculty of Dean Marty's university.

The point is that such attitudes are so deeply ingrained and so unquestionably held by the New York liberal intellectual establishment (and particularly by its Jewish component) that they have become undiscussable assumptions. Not all intellectuals and not all Jews, of course, share these assumptions, and some even reject them. Adam Walinsky, for example, broke the conspiracy of silence about liberal anti-Catholicism in a pro-parochial school article in *The New Republic*.

There are, however, four million Catholics in New York City, seven million in New York state, and fifty million in the whole republic. A liberal Democratic candidate who thinks he can win without them can't add.

Either the liberal intellectual elite, that dominates the Democratic party in New York and aspires to do so nationally, will face up to its own nativist assumptions and ignorance and begin learning what the Catholic population is really like, or it will keep on losing elections. To put Catholics on tickets would be a nice beginning, but Catholics, however ignorant and superstitious they may appear, can spot window dressing. A token Catholic won't get you very many votes. But Catholics are conservative aren't they? They believe in such ridiculous retrograde values as family, neighborhood, and country. How can good liberals make alliances with such people? Alas for the good liberals, most Americans believe in those values too—and a lot of them are far more conservative on economics and race than Catholics.

Liberal self-righteousness is impenetrable. Eventually they will understand Catholic *power,* a power which is very slow to organize itself mostly because of the incompetence of ecclesiastical leaders. But Hesburgh is one of the few effective ones, and after chewing the hide off church dignitaries who worry about abortion and not about famine or war, he issued the following warning:

Last year is last year, but memories remain. The next time, I expect that Catholics will have better leadership, will be more highly politicized, more conscious of their inherent strength, less ready to be promised help by a President who, once he had their votes, hardly lifted a finger to help them or their two causes. The Catholics could well learn from Jewish leadership which also wanted two things last year and achieved both of them: massive aid to Israel and denial of trade favor to Russia until emigration is liberalized.*

In the meantime, New Yorkers apparently have to face the possibility of choosing between people like Bella Abzug and James Buckley. And from the secure perspective of Daley-land, represented in the United States Senate by Adlai Stevenson and in the House by a black, I will observe that it serves you liberal nativist so-and-sos right if you never win another election.

*Ibid., p. 20.

section two *Resources for the*
Communal
Catholic

CHAPTER SIX

The Big Opportunities

So the communal Catholic—the Catholic who is certain in his gut, if unsure in his head, must deal with an inept church, incorrigibly romantic intellectuals, and bigoted non-Catholics. He does not have easy access to either a clear description of his past or a concise summary of his world view. But he knows the past is important and he intuits that the world view is basically sound. He also suspects, though he would be hard put to articulate why, that the world view is, if not exactly "relevant," at least opportune—indeed, more opportune that it has been for a long time.

He couldn't be more right—though, perhaps for fear of what he might find, he is cautious about pursuing his suspicion too far.

At any given point in its history the prospects for the church have been a mingling of light and dark, opportunities and problems. Whether one chooses to focus on the light or the dark is probably more a function of one's own psychology or hormone balance, or the state of one's sex life, than it is of the reflection of the complexities, the uncertainties, the confusions, and, above all, the possibilities of the real world in which the church must struggle. I should like to suggest that in the present cultural milieu in the United States there are seven opportunities for the church, not only to respond effectively to the communal Catholic but to the world at large. I shall highlight six of those opportunities in this chapter, turn to the seventh in the next chapter—the Catholic Ethic—and more deeply discuss the others in some of the chapters that follow.

Taken together, these opportunities probably make this one of the most important strategic moments in the last several hundred years of church history. That such opportunities exist does not mean that they will be seized; to point out opportunities is not to assure success. Indeed, if anything is to be made of the opportunities I will describe, it will take more effort, intelligence, and discipline than American Catholicism has displayed in the present century. I present this case not to refute those who say the church will continue to deteriorate. I merely refute those who say there is no reason why it should not continue to deteriorate.

The most important issue facing American culture today is the issue of human nature and sinfulness. The word sin may seldom be used, although when Karl Menninger writes a book asking whatever happened to it, one begins to suspect that perhaps even the word may become acceptable again. But the issue of the goodness or evilness of humankind is more explicit than ever since the time of Voltaire. The new prophets of doom, such as Robert Heilbroner in *An Inquiry into the Human Prospect,* Richard Goodwin, Konrad Lorenz, and a whole host of lesser figures, are propounding apocalypse. Loren Eiseley has summarized the viewpoint of these neo-Manicheans with the announcement (to me, incredibly arrogant) that the evolutionary process made a disastrous mistake when it produced humankind. The prophecies of doom may occasionally have the trappings of science, usually economics or ecology (as in the case of the now disgraced Club of Rome report, *Limits to Growth.*) But in fact they are not economic or biological writings at all, they are *theological.* The doom they see impending is one based not so much on biological or economic projections as on despair over human nature. As the critics at the University of Sussex make clear in their evaluation of *Limits to Growth,* one has merely to build into their world model a relatively small technological improvement and the whole thrust of the model is reversed. Heilbroner is quite explicitly searching for symbols, settling genially for Prometheus and Atlas, two symbols that never meant much to the Greeks and probably mean less to contemporary human beings. (Heilbroner is apparently unaware that there is another symbol system that had some contribution to make to Western culture.)

The intellectual and cultural elites of the United States, indeed of the whole Western world, have shifted from naive Lockean Pelagianism to neo-Manicheism. Humankind is innately aggressive and destructive, we are told, and barring a profound transformation of human nature we will destroy ourselves and the planet. Whether this aggressiveness is built into our personalities, as Lorenz would argue, or whether it was acquired when we became hunters, as Sherwood Washburn has suggested, is scarcely the point. Humankind is destructive of its own fellows, its world, and itself; it is predestined (and I use the word advisedly) to snuff out the evolutionary process, of which mankind itself presently seems to be the crowning achievement. (On a more popular level, note how many science fiction stories assume a post-apocalypse world. In the case of Philip Jose Farmer's *Stone God Awakens,* the world has been destroyed by inhabitants of other worlds who have become afraid that humankind will destroy the universe.)

Enlightenment rationalism is in disarray and retreat. Science is no longer to be the source of salvation; and the Christian churches, once assailed, assaulted, and abused because they were not scientific enough, now find themselves blamed for the disaster that science and technology have inflicted on the cosmos. With the wisdom of old age, (approaching senility, perhaps) Lewis Mumford tells us we are in a new "Dark Ages," and Arnold Toynbee blames all our troubles on the book of Genesis. (Moses apparently invented the steam engine, the internal combustion engine, and the atomic bomb.)

One must view Erich Fromm's brilliant volume on the nature of human aggressiveness as a last-ditch defense of Enlightenment hopefulness. Just as Loren Eiseley and Robert Heilbroner may be the first of the new Manichees, Fromm is the last of the old Pelagians.

It may well be that the terms of the controversy about the nature of

human nature are unduly narrow. They are still part of the legacy that
Western culture has inherited from Augustine, whose troubled soul
continues to haunt us. Is human nature totally bad, as Manes whispered in Augustine's right ear, or is it fundamentally good, as the
good Irish monk Pelagius whispered in his left ear? Heilbroner and
Fromm may not realize it but they are only echoes of the murmurings
of Augustine's intellectual seducers.

There is, of course, and always has been among American intellectual and cultural elites, a predisposition to Manicheism. The Puri-
tan Protestant view of human nature has been locked in conflict with
the much more hopeful view of human nature that one finds in the
Federalist Papers and in de Toqueville since this country was settled.
The men who founded our republic had seen the failure of the republics of virtue that were supposed to have been established by the state
constitutions and the Articles of Confederation. They were under no
illusions. James Madison, in the tenth and fifty-first Federalist Papers, can hardly be written off as a naive enthusiast. This strain of
American cultural tradition is surely at odds with the grim, one might
say, sour view of the Protestant tradition which reached its culmina-
tion in Reinhold Niebuhr's classic, *The Nature and Destiny of Man*.
Man may not be totally depraved or totally corrupt, in Niebuhr's
view of things, but he is damn near it. Niebuhr casually wrote off the
Catholic position, as propounded, for example, by Aquinas, as
"semi-Pelagianism." (I will confess that I have always found semi-
Pelagianism a consoling position.)

Protestant liberalism may occasionally incline to abandon such a
despondent view of human nature, as it did in the glory days of the
secular theology in the early 1960s; but it always seems to end up
back in Niebuhr's camp. What is happening presently, however, is
that Protestants and agnostics alike have moved far to the right of
Niebuhr, making him look almost semi-Pelagianistic. (After all,
Niebuhr believed in salvation, and Heilbroner, Eiseley, and Goodwin do not.)

Make no mistake about it. This debate about the nature of human
nature, still carried on in obscure journals and learned books, is the

most decisive cultural battle of our time. The Catholic tradition has spent most of the last several hundred years jousting with Enlightenment Pelagianism and fighting an occasional rear guard action with what we take to be the Protestant semi-Manicheism. The Pelagians are gone, my friends, and even the semi-Manichees like Niebuhr are being written off as benighted optimists. The Catholic view summarized in our theology books, that man might be deprived but not depraved, now looks benign beyond belief—literally beyond belief. The irony of the situation, of course, is that there are hardly any Catholic theologians today who are reflecting on the nature of human nature or, if you wish, on the nature of human sinfulness. As in so many other opportunities of the cultural moment, we vaguely suspect (at least some of us do) that there might be something in our tradition which could inform the present dialogue. What we might contribute is rather close to what may be found in the tenth and fifty-first Federalist Papers. But we are hard put to verbalize what the Catholic tradition is. Perhaps too many theologians have been marching on picket lines instead of marking their theology books.

The second area of opportunity is in the definition of pluralism. Whatever one may think of the so-called ethnic revival there can be no doubt that American culture is more aware of its own diversity now than it has been for at least the last half century. In addition, perhaps for the first time ever, we are finally ready to accept the legitimacy of diversity, if we are not yet ready to acknowledge its richness and its promise. The principal reason for the new legitimacy of pluralism is the black cultural revival of the 1960s. If black is beautiful and if brown is beautiful, then there is no reason why Polish should not be beautiful or Italian or Czech or Irish.

Some of our intellectual and cultural arbiters are willing to concede the rights of cultural diversity to blacks but not to white ethnic groups because to recognize cultural diversity in the latter groups would encourage divisiveness. Black nationalism, it would seem, is not divisive; Polish and Irish nationalism is. However, the so-called ethnics might be excused for not seeing the logic of this argument.

In fact, most of the integrationists and assimilationists who caved in to the black militants of the 1950s and the 1960s did not realize what they were surrendering to. They felt that the new cultural pride of the blacks was the same thing as the black separatism preached by a few far out black kooks. But they never distinguished between pluralism and separatism, between cultural pride and opting out of the society. In fact, as the overwhelming burden of the empirical evidence indicates, blacks don't want out of American society; they want into it as respectable, legitimate, powerful participators. What really happened in the 1960s is that both culturally and politically blacks began to act like an ethnic group. The black mayors of Newark, Cleveland, Detroit, Dayton, Atlanta, Los Angeles, and Gary have proved themselves masters at the art of ethnic coalition politics.

A third critical cultural issue in the United States is that of values. One hears it in every foundation office on Manhattan Island, and one hears it (though in muted whispers) in many government agencies. Government bureaucrats are not sure but what it might be un-American, or at least a violation of the separation of church and state, to talk about values. The value crisis should come as no surprise. When Lockean hopefulness about human nature and melting pot assimilationism collapsed within the same decade, the Pandora's box was opened on values. Make no mistake, these issues are far more important than those of marijuana, amnesty, feminism, and sexual liberation. (Amnesty has been an issue before in American society—and has always won, by the way.) Ingesting chemicals into the bloodstream was an ancient American practice. Feminism was not thought up in the late 1960s, although it surely experienced rebirth then. One need not know much American history to know that sexual permissiveness was argued seriously by many of the utopians of the past, and vigorously practiced in most American rural and farm communities.

The questioning of far more basic values, those that have to do with one's picture of the nature of human nature and the nature of human society, are what really gave rise to the crisis of values. And when one begins to wonder about the nature of the human and his society, then one wonders about life and death, good and evil, love and hatred, work and leisure, family and community. It is all well and good to talk about revolution, future shock, and the new permissiveness. It turns out that one cannot live by antivalues. Having shucked off the values of the past (or, more specifically, by having persuaded himself that he has shucked them off), a young person finds himself still needing a set of convictions about the nature of the world, life, society, and himself. One of the things we are noting on the college campuses today is that whatever can be said of the lost generation of the 1960s, the found generation of the 1970s seems to have values strikingly like those of its parents.

Still, even though the generation gap is mostly myth, the crisis of confidence that has shaken American intellectual and cultural elites, since the death of John Kennedy, let us say, is real enough. These elites existed a long time on the accumulated capital of the Western cultural tradition, with its Jewish, Christian, and Greek components. They were able even to deny some of the fundamental premises of the Western cultural tradition and still maintain its values. The shock of the 1960s may be ebbing somewhat, but it revealed to many of our cultural and intellectual leaders how thin the basis of their secular-scientific-liberal-rationalist-humanitarian-agnostic world view was. They are scrambling around looking for other values to give purpose to their lives, to pass on to their children, and to hold the society together. The orgy of anti-intellectual romanticism in which the old turned to the young for cultural guidance during the 1960s was the first phase of the horrified reaction of the liberal rationalists when they discovered that liberal rationalism was in grave trouble. Unfortunately, the new messianic group of Consciousness III young people proved no more stable as a political and social elite than did the cold-war liberals. The question of what, if anything, human life means (and that is the ultimate value question) is now more open than it has ever been in the history of the United States, and perhaps more open than since the beginning of the Enlightenment.

And this issue of values, now so poignant in American society, gives us an opportunity to weigh into the dialogue with our Catholic symbol system. Not everyone will embrace them, but damn it all, our symbols properly presented, deserve a hearing. When Harvey Cox sings hymns of praise to the Virgin of Guadalupe, the Catholic symbol system is, or at least could be, alive and well and living in Cambridge. The symbols are not easy magic answers of the sort that used to be deduced from papal encyclicals. Anyone who tries to derive answers from symbols doesn't know what a symbol is. Instead of parsing and analyzing the symbol, one "puts it on" and plays around within its densely packed polyvalent, multilayered richness. Then, looking at the world through the illumination furnished by the prisms of the symbol, one finds not answers so much as a new view. Curiously enough, just when Robert Heilbroner is looking for symbols we are being told by some of our own self-confessed thinkers that Catholic symbols are irrelevant, anachronistic. I am not suggesting that Catholic Christianity properly interpreted in our time will win the Heilbroners of the world to our side. I fear that Mr. Heilbroner, Mr. Goodwin, Mr. Eiseley, and the rest enjoy the present fashion of despair far too much to be won away from it.

A fourth area of cultural concern that presents the church with immense opportunity is sexuality. The family, we are told, may be disappearing from the scene. Don't you believe it. What is unique is not that young people are having sexual relations before marriage; such behavior is as old as the human race. What is unique about our time is that such behavior is now justified—apparently honestly and seriously—on the grounds that it helps young people to make sure that the commitment they make to one another in a marriage is a wise one. Trial marriage is justified, not on the grounds that sexual intercourse without responsibility is fun, but that it is a useful and helpful preparation for marriage.

Similarly, multiple forms of marital infidelity, currently obtaining so much attention in the Sunday supplements, are almost always justified on the grounds that they enhance the relationship between husband and wife. Open marriage, free marriage, or "swinging" are supported not on the grounds that infidelity and promiscuity provide one with a hell of a good time but rather on the grounds that for many complex (and dubious) psychological reasons "comarital" sex reinforces the relationship between husband and wife. (Dr. Bartel in his responsible anthropological study of the matter suggests that, in fact, swinging is another form of male exploitation imposed on the wife, who may be more or less willing but goes along with it because she recognizes her husband's need to act out his adolescent fantasies.)

And one of the most powerful arguments advanced in favor of women's lib is that the "new equality" between husband and wife will provide a richer and more meaningful relationship in the family. Hardly a single paperback book on deviant forms of marriage (with the possible exception of such madcap communitarian sexual fantasies as *The Harrad Experiment*) does not conclude with some sort of ritual and dramatic reference to "new, deeper, and richer relationships between man and woman."

The real problem is not so much that the family is falling apart but that our expectations of the physical and psychological rewards of family life are growing far more rapidly than our capacities to deal with the challenges and problems of human intimacy. For most people divorce comes not because they no longer believe in marriage but because they no longer feel that what they want out of marriage can be obtained from the relationship in which they find themselves; and virtually all divorced people attempt once again (with perhaps more patience and tolerance if not more success) a traditional marital relationship.

Paradoxically, the structures of society no longer reinforce the relationship between husband and wife, parents and child. Separate careers (or one career and one commitment, more or less voluntary, to the home), the absence of joint economic effort, the establishment of close relationships with professional colleagues, the excitement and challenge of the world beyond the family, the uneven rhythm of life-cycle changes—all of these leave the marital relationship pretty much dependent on the psychological and physical bond between husband and wife. Unless both partners are willing to be patient, generous, open, and forgiving, the strain on the bond is certainly going to be intense—even more so when ideology is at hand to justify punitive, aggressive, and destructive behavior (whether that ideology be old fashioned religion or new fashioned feminism). It may well be that the problem with the marriage is not that it is no longer important but that it is too important. With the exceptions of a handful of people in sexual communes, the relationship between a man and a woman more or less permanently committed to one another and usually with children attached is going to continue to be for most people in American society (at least) the most important single dimension of their lives. The basic cultural issue is not whether the family will be replaced but how human beings can grow in the skills of trusting and generous intimacy.

The Catholic tradition and symbol system is not without resources in this matter, although currently we are so busy worrying about birth control, celibacy, and divorce that we seem unable to mobilize our resources to speak to more basic issues. One can take it for granted that most sex will be between a husband and wife, if only because economic and logistic reasons make it difficult to maintain a mistress or a lover on a sustained basis in contemporary America. The question for the church is: What can it do to sustain and enrich the sexual and human relationship between a husband and wife? Again, it seems to me that the issue is more open and the opportunity greater than ever before in recent memory—and perhaps, at least as far as sex and the family goes, more open and more challenging than ever before in human history.

Yet another opportunity is provided for the church by the relatively surprising honesty that has developed in recent years on the subject of death. The social scientists and medical researchers who have devoted serious attention to the subject of aging (which begins at twenty-one, I am told), the crisis of the middle years, dying, and death have opened up culture perspectives which in more naive times were firmly closed. The fact of death was prettied over on the one hand by the elaborate rituals of the funeral parlor and the cemetery and on the other by happy talk about cures for cancer and heart disease. While most of us had not gone quite so far down the line towards Christian Science as the French press, which seems reluctant to discuss fatal illness, we did our best to repress and to hide whenever possible thoughts of aging, sickness, dying, and death. Hospital researchers have discovered that, oddly enough, the M.D.'s were often the worst offenders, refusing to discuss death with terminally ill patients not because it would harm the patient so much as it would disturb the doctor. My own doctor tells me that the battery of tests I take every year are available free to all the M.D.'s on the staff of his hospital, and only a minority ever bother to take them. Why, after all, should doctors be any different from the rest of us? Aging, death, and dying are as difficult for them to face as for anyone else.

Death is out in the open again, and the crisis of the middle years, fundamentally a crisis of coming to terms with our own mortality, is increasingly seen as the decisive turning point in a person's life. It is now not only permissible but fashionable to talk about the meaning of life and death. Furthermore, as an ever increasing proportion of the population goes through psychotherapy, the fundamental death fear that lurks in our personalities is smoked out into the open and faced at a much earlier age in life. For those who take psychotherapy as something more than a pleasant game to be played occasionally, the therapeutic experience itself is a form of death—leading, of course, to rebirth. But in the therapeutic experience (if it is anything more than a game-playing, casual encounter) the awesome twin realities of life and death are faced in a terrifying and frequently brutal fashion. We are born with two diseases: life, which is invariably fatal, and hope, which suggests that death may not be the final word.

It is hardly necessary to suggest that Catholic Christianity may have symbols available that would be pertinent to our newly explicit cultural concern about death. It should also be unnecessary to suggest that our position is *not* that there is a "life after death." The Christian position does not deny the awful, ugly, evil reality of death. It does not offer cheap and easy consolation to those caught in the anticipated death anguish of the middle years. Christianity is a religion of the cross, and the cross was an instrument of death. The easy, simple, facile "life after death" response may be appropriate in some religions but not for the religion of the cross.

But Christianity does say that the cross does not have the last word, that hope is not foolish, that death is not the ultimate reality. It doesn't say much more than this, and it certainly offers no detailed and elaborate pictures of an afterlife such as other-world religions provide; it merely assures us that our hopes are not in vain and the power of God's love will triumph over death for us just as it triumphed over death for Jesus. This is not much to cling to when one is growing old or beginning to die. It is nonetheless the best realistic hope that humankind has ever been offered. It is realistic because it does not deny the ugliness of death, and it is hopeful because it assures us that, as Gregory Baum has noted, "tomorrow will be different" even when tomorrow is the day following the last one in our lives.

The sixth opportunity for the church is that of mysticism. I do not mean counterculture mysticism, psychedelic mysticism, drug-induced mysticism, or even mysticism pursued by those enthusiastic young people who shave their heads, don saffron colored robes, and engage in various strange (though apparently on occasion effective) oriental ascetic practices. The research that my colleague William McCready and I have done in recent years indicates beyond doubt that a considerable number of Americans have had mystical experiences that are neither drug-induced nor part of some counterculture freakout. It is also our impression that the proportion of people in the population who have had such experiences is relatively constant, and that the so-called mystical revival is a reawakening of awareness of the mystic dimensions of human life. While it is unlikely that many Americans will turn to Eastern religions, in which mystical ecstasy is the primary goal of existence, it is likely that large numbers of Americans will become much more open and aware of the mystic dimensions of everyday life. (Let me make it clear that I write about mystical experiences, but I do not have them.)

As the institution which has presided over the oldest mystical tradition in the Western world, the Roman Church ought not to be without resources on this issue. I am always intrigued by those Catholic enthusiasts of yoga and Transcendental Meditation who seem unaware of Richard Rolle of Hampole, Juliana of Norwich, Meister Eckhardt, Teresa of Avila, Juan de la Cruz (who is *not* the third baseman of the Pittsburgh Pirates), and even Ignatius of Loyola. I remember being astonished at a meeting where Charles Davis (that folk hero of the Catholic left) denied any Catholic mystical tradition and asked me what I meant by it. When I reeled off the list of Catholic mystics he had no response. Mind you, I have nothing against either yoga or Transcendental Meditation, and I wouldn't even contend that John of the Cross's "dark night of the soul" is superior to Eastern mysticism, but it seems obvious to me that it does say something not said elsewhere in the world and which ought to be said with great vigor to those naive enthusiasts of the current mystical revival.

There is one aspect of Christian mysticism that ought to be especially pertinent. Christian mysticism is activist in the sense that however much the Christian may withdraw from society he does not view his experience as an end in itself. Indeed, the "stuff" of the Christian religion is not individual experiences but relationships. One does not see ecstasy so much as service of the Lord as he is found in the least of the brothers. Christian mysticism is not a cop-out mysticism; it is not a turning away from the political, social, and human problems of ·the world we live in. The late Thomas Merton, perhaps the most famous American mystic of our time, was anything but uninvolved in the world around him—whether one happened to agree or disagree with the emphases of his involvement. That mystical experience is the source of and reinforcement for social action is a uniquely

Christian—or perhaps I should say Yahwistic—religious insight. In contemporary America, however, some of the enthusiasts of the mystical revival are deliberately and consciously turning to mysticism as an alternative to failed political action.

To say that there are more opportunities for the church in the present cultural and social situation than there have been in the two decades since I have become a priest, and perhaps (a heroic leap) more opportunities than in the last two centuries, is not to imply that we are sitting pretty or that our work will be easy or that the opportunities will be as automatic as a home run by Babe Ruth. It is merely to suggest that there are opportunities. If there are no grounds for easy optimism—and presumably at this stage of the post conciliar disillusionment there are no optimists left—neither are there grounds for despair. The opportunities are there: complex, knotty, difficult.

My list is not exhaustive; others may have a different list, others may think of things I have omitted. We have had more than enough three-, five-, or seven-point programs. If I have left some of your favorite challenges off the list, the reason may be my deficiencies of vision or that I have tried to grapple with the most fundamental "core" issues. If, for example, I do not list the race question on my agenda, it is not because I believe it to be of less than utmost importance for American society but because I think it can be subsumed and should be wrestled with under the broader, deeper, and more difficult issue (at least intellectually difficult) of cultural pluralism.

CHAPTER SEVEN

The "Catholic Ethic" and Social Policy

Of all the hunches he has, the communal Catholic is most likely to be stubborn about the nature of human nature. Everything in his childhood experience in family and neighborhood leads him to believe that human nature is more good than evil, but still pretty evil. He believes you can trust people—sometimes and up to a point. He does not think, as do many of his Protestant friends, that humankind is basically evil and must be coerced into virtue by fear and guilt, but neither does he believe, like his socialist friends, that you can remake human nature completely. He distrusts great reform projects, grand designs, and completely new starts; he tends to believe that progress does occur, but not always, and when it does, only as a result of organic growth rather than wiping the slate clean. He is therefore very ill at ease with most of the assumptions of social policy that he hears around him. But true to his own pragmatic instincts, he goes right ahead with social ventures, leaving to others the abstract and theoretical reflections on what they mean. It has been his observation that if a policy works, the abstractions don't matter, and if it doesn't, the abstracter looks pretty foolish.

Daniel P. Moynihan, Ambassador to the U.N., has addressed himself to a discussion of the transition from the "utilitarian ethic" to the "therapeutic ethic" in the formulation of social policy. The

fundamental assumption of the utilitarian ethic, Moynihan says, is
that "man is acquisitive and aggressive, but men may cooperate out
of self-interest, and social arrangements can be adopted which encourage such cooperation." Man is rational "even though slow to
perceive where rational interest resides." Moynihan continues: "Social policy in such a setting defines itself fairly readily. The state
should intervene in social arrangements mainly to restore or maintain
the equilibrium of a largely self-regulating system: to intervene so as
to attain a minimum of intervention."

The utilitarian ethic, Moynihan argues, did *not* mean a ritual
avoidance of government action. It was a liberal British government
in 1911 which introduced unemployment insurance to the modern
world, for example. Safety and health legislation, pure-food laws,
anti-monopoly legislation all represented forms of government intervention to ensure that the system worked. Still, according to Moynihan, interventions were future oriented. "It was the prospect of good
or bad consequences which shaped behavior, because man—being
reasonable—would choose pleasurable consequences over disagree-
able ones."

But there is another ethic which views human behavior as shaped
not by consequent future events but by past ones. The therapeutic
ethic assumes that human behavior is not reasonable, that it is controlled by events that have already occurred, particularly in childhood. Social policy, therefore, is to be oriented to respond to the
problems created by a childhood-produced "frustration-aggressive"
syndrome. (In his article, Moynihan analyzes the important influence
of John Dollard's book *Frustration and Aggression,* published in
1939.) Crime, urban unrest, world conflict, social upheaval in general were the result of the frustration of various minority groups. Unless a massive effort were undertaken by government to change these
conditions, aggression would continue to mount. So the argument
ran that unless the Vietnam war were ended, students would tear up
the campuses; unless racial inequality were eliminated, blacks would
tear up the cities; unless the problem of hunger were solved, the poor

nations would develop atomic bombs to drop on New York. The therapeutic ethic is one of the two principal arguments in the repertoire of social activists (the other being an appeal to the guilt of the oppressing majorities).

In the utilitarian world view, government intervened intermittently—though perhaps powerfully—to maintain a balance among selfish but reasonable men. In the therapeutic world view, government intervenes massively and systematically to correct injustices that lead to frustrations which in turn lead to destructive behavior from nonrational, not to say irrational, men. The therapeutic world view, Moynihan notes, has triumphed almost completely among social policy makers.

Both the utilitarian and thereapeutic ethics are fundamentally "Protestant" in the Weberian sense and also in a broader philosophical sense. They both assume the isolated individual working against the rest of society. In the utilitarian ethic he vigorously seeks his own good; in the therapeutic ethic he rages against society's oppressions. In both cases, however, a rather grim (thoroughly Lutheran) view of both human nature and society is operative. In the utilitarian ethic humankind is fundamentally selfish, but fortunately that selfishness works for the good. In the therapeutic ethic humankind is fundamentally aggressive, and his aggression when frustrated builds up to explosion point.

In both ethics society is oppressive. In the utilitarian ethic society must be held in check so that it does not interfere with the free working of individual selfishness. In the therapeutic, society must be restrained either by court order or by moralistic appeal to guilt from continuing to frustrate the aspirations of the frustrated group (unionists, blacks, students, women, homosexuals, etc.). This view, Protestant in origin (or perhaps Augustinian) and funneled through Hobbes, is so much a part of the American intellectual and cultural milieu that both our right- and our left-wing social ethics implicitly share the same fundamental assumption of the lonely, frustrated, self-seeking individual struggling against the great leviathan society. Even most

American Marxists—and no one sounds more Protestant than an American Marxist—seem to share this assumption. While social class may be for the Marxist an important analytic category, it is not something to which one *belongs* in anything but the ideological sense.

A different perspective is provided by what I call, perhaps chauvinistically, the "Catholic ethic." Catholics share it to some considerable extent with the Jews and with the European and Latin American Marxists, but it is still fair to call this alternative ethic "Catholic" because Catholics are surely the largest group in America to hold it (however unconsciously they may do so).

The Catholic ethic is to be found in its high tradition in the papal encyclicals (which of course no one reads anymore, and perhaps that is just as well). In its low tradition it may be found in the neighborhoods, the precincts, the union locals. The Catholic ethic takes a much more benign view of both humankind and society than either the utilitarian or therapeutic ethic. Like our founding fathers, it is willing to trust human freedom up to a point, not because it thinks that individual selfishness will lead to group utility, but because it believes that in addition to being competitive man is also cooperative, particularly when he is not threatened. This benign view of human nature is also dubious about the virtue of compulsion inherent in the therapeutic ethic. It is more inclined to effect social reform by cooperation and consensus than by messianic appeals to moral transformation or by Supreme Court decision. It believes that humankind is good enough to respond to the gradualist approach, and it doubts the apocalyptic warnings that frustrated groups will tear society apart. Here again it has a much more benign view of the sense and sensibility of even frustrated groups than does the Protestant-therapeutic ethic.

It believes further that social groups contribute to and are essential for the growth of the individual person and that they do not stand over and against the person as oppressors. From the standpoint of the Catholic ethic—one might as well call it the "communitarian" or "communal" ethic—humans exist as integrated members of social communities, those tribes, clans, neighborhoods, ethnic groups, churches, unions, business associations, governmental groups which intervene between the isolated individual and the social mass. It is through the interaction of members of these groups, particularly insofar as membership overlaps, that the patterns of social structure emerge and that the *institutions for social reform* are brought into being. One creates a better society not by law, fiat, religious conversion, or the promotion of individual selfishness. One creates it by changing the patterns of relationship—a tedious, time consuming, gradualistic process, and one that frequently goes on without the intervention of any higher order groups (a dictum that was reflected in the papal doctrine of "subsidiary function").

While the Catholic ethic does flow logically from the Catholic view of humankind and human society, it does not flow either uniquely or inevitably from that world view. Not all Catholics practice the communal ethic, and many who are not Catholics do practice it. The pragmatism of the Anglo-Saxon political tradition, the volunteerism and the American propensity to found private organizations to achieve private or quasi-public goals, the frontier experience, the necessities of day to day politics and administration have all led to a political and social "style" very different from either the utilitarian or the therapeutic ethic as described in the Moynihan address.

The Catholic ethic is not a textbook ethic. It is an *a posteriori* ethic concerned neither with grand designs nor with utopias (despite Thomas More). It is far more concerned with the realities of the local situation in which one finds oneself than with splendid intellectual designs of the sort Professor Galbraith and his cronies spin on a late evening in Cambridge. It emphasizes the importance of family and neighborhood, grass roots relationships, loyalty, friendship, and trust, because it believes that these are attributes of the "socialness" of man's nature. It is very skeptical of grand designs, ideology, and apocalypse, because at the grass roots level grand designs do not fit, ideology seems to be irrelevant (as Geno Baroni puts it, it doesn't get the sidewalk fixed), and apocalypse never seems to occur.

The Catholic ethic is at work in American society. In both the trade union movement and the urban political organization—even as these two institutions become black—the Catholic or communal ethic is alive and well. Moynihan is perfectly correct, of course, in excluding it from his article (save for his oblique reference to papal encyclicals) because the Catholic ethic has never underpinned the self-conscious making of social policy; but it has nonetheless exercised a considerable influence in American society. Few serious observers of American trade unionism would think that the communalism of the unions (so far as it still exists at this late date) owes more to its Marxist-Jewish component than it does to its Catholic component. There used to be an argument in intellectual Catholic circles about whether Catholic trade union leaders were influenced by the social encyclicals. On the one hand it seemed that they stood for much the same things that the encyclicals espoused; on the other hand it was not at all clear that they ever bothered to read them. In fact, they didn't have to read the encyclicals because they already knew the ethic. They learned it in the communities in which they grew up.

Implicit, unnoticed, unappreciated, the Catholic ethic is nonetheless still around. And the most important difference between it and the utilitarian and therapeutic ethics is that it works. It has been used by the urban political organizations which have provided the electoral muscle for the New Deal for the last forty years; it has produced a trade union movement which contributed more to the health and happiness of the working class than all the socialist elements in the world combined; it is responsible for the most organizationally sound form of Catholicism that humankind has evern known (the proportion of Catholics receiving weekly communion has doubled in the last ten years, for example).

Each of the new immigrant groups that has entered American society climbed its way up the ladder of urban political power and eventual economic success by virtue of the Catholic ethic at work. And it is working for the blacks. As one young black student said to me, "The Cook County organization provides a higher proportion of jobs for blacks than any other institution in the state of Illinois." The ethic has generated more change in attitudes on racial prejudice than all the McGovern-type moralism in the world. Thus, for example, one third of the Catholics of the country live in integrated housing, and two thirds of the Catholic school children go to integrated schools. Surely an ethic that has these sorts of achievements to its credit deserves more than short shrift when American social policy makers sit down to wonder about what comes next.

I have wondered for some time why social policy makers and Catholic intellectuals (so-called) have ignored the findings of Terry N. Clark which show a massive correlation (.6) between the proportion of Catholics in a city and the level of public expenditures. Professor Clark's research seems to establish beyond any reasonable doubt both the existence of a Catholic ethic and its benign influence on urban problems. For those unfamiliar with his work, it should be emphasized that Professor Clark, like the good sociologist he is, tried every conceivable intervening variable to make the correlations go away, and he could not find one. Recently (in a personal communication), he suggested that it was now time to accept the existence of a Catholic ethic and to begin exploring its origins.

Can the Catholic ethic make a new contribution to social policy? There was a time when Catholics had all the answers to social policy issues. These were derived syllogistically from papal encyclicals and were incorporated into the various three-, five-, and seven-year plans of group discussion that characterized the Catholic action movements of the fifties, as well as in the "industry council plan" that was the rallying cry of the Catholic social action movement in the same decade. It is difficult to believe that two thousand years of accumulated tradition and a characteristic view of human nature cannot make a worthy contribution to the American social policy debate. Furthermore, if Catholicism is reduced to being a minor partner of the official liberal establishment, applauding and legitimating its social policy premises, it is scarcely in any position to criticize those premises—unless, of course, it goes over to the other side and engages in a critique from the Marxist viewpoint à la liberation theology. Such a critique may be fun but, as Geno Baroni notes, it is quite irrelevant to things like getting better schools, better housing, and better transportation in the real world of American society today.

The question is not whether there are some unique and special Catholic answers to the problems of society; the question should be whether there is a unique contribution that the Catholic tradition in general and the American Catholic experience in particular can make to social policy formation.

The fundamental issue of social policy which the Catholic ethic must address is whether government intervention is the only way to produce effective changes in the social structure. The McGovern movement, for all its claim to represent a resurgence of populism, was in fact a collection of the same old tired New Deal clichés: more government programs, more government intervention, and more governmental control. As I read the literature of the neoegalitarians who think they are shaping the political issues of the future, I am dismayed to find that they are in fact blindly demanding even more government intervention. The socialist ideal of a government running as much as possible springs forth perennially despite the failures of socialist governments all over the world. One need not limit oneself merely to the Soviet Union. Visit India to discover how bankrupt and incompetent socialism can be.

At a time when government-run education has become almost worthless, government-run postal service totally undependable, government-administered police unable to cope with crime (resulting in private security and police forces which provide income for cops to do in their off duty hours what the bureaucratic structures prevent them from doing during working hours), when one must tangle with the Federal Energy Office, the Internal Revenue Service, the Small Business Administration, and a host of other officious, incompetent, and oppressive government structures, when the complex of political disgraces subsumed under the label "Watergate" shows how unprincipled men can put government bureaucracy to their own uses with precious little resistance from the bureaucrats, it scarcely seems per-

tinent or appealing to suggest yet more government intervention. But
in fact the liberal left wing of the Democratic party has no other ideas
about how social policy can be formulated and implemented.

The people are fed up. Opposition to big government is as prevalent in the population among those of the left as it is among those of
the right. In the National Opinion Research Center's (NORC) study
of American political history over the last twenty years, opposition to
big government is no longer a predictor of a right wing stance on any
other issue. Support of big government is no longer a predictor of a
left wing stance either. The intellectual and cultural elites have yet to
catch up with the rest of the population.

There is also the melancholy problem that some of the best inten-
tioned social interventions of one era produce the worst problems of
the next. The population explosion in many countries is due to the
public health intervention which led to a decrease in the death rate
when there was no commensurate effort to produce a decrease in the
birth rate. In the United States the welfare legislation of the 1930s,
certainly the most benign and enlightened social interventions of the
time, has produced perhaps the most serious domestic problem in the
country, that of welfare dependency. Because this now vicious and
evil welfare system was institutionalized in a government program, it
will be difficult if not impossible to reform. And just try to reform the
Internal Revenue Service! The Service with its insane Form 1040 and
its investigative agents and their "quotas of productivity" is itself the
result of another benign and enlightened social intervention, the
progressive tax.

There is little disposition in most quarters to return to the era of
Herbert Hoover. There are some things that government does well,
especially the transfer of funds. There are some other things it does
moderately well—building aircraft carriers, hospitals, and moon
rockets. And there are other things it does very badly, such as trying
to intervene with programs to benefit families and local communities.

We can distill from this discussion three critical social policy questions:

1. How does one make existing government agencies responsive and responsible? In the old days one dealt with government through the precinct captain. One had something the captain wanted, a vote, and he damn well better deliver efficient service or he might lose it. The Social Security Administration bureaucrat needs absolutely nothing from his client, and whether he delivers efficient, courteous, and responsible service is a matter of complete indifference to him.

2. How does one phase out social policy programs and interventions that are not working or are counterproductive without exercising the Congressional meat axe or engaging in bureaucratic infighting? (I sometimes think that half of the working time of Washington bureaucrats is devoted to protecting their existence against the attacks and incursions of other bureaucrats.) In the old days the political boss could simply announce that the program was over and it was over.

3. Most importantly, where can we get a whole new perspective on social policy in which the public welfare is promoted and the rights and happiness of minority groups defended, protected, and enhanced without at the same time turning over larger segments of our lives to government control? There have been many suggestions as to what might be done about the intolerable power of the multinational oil companies, for example, but so far as I know, no one has suggested that the Sherman Antitrust Act might be enforced.

Now let's turn to our original question. Does Catholicism have any contribution to make to social policy discussions? Is there anything in either the Catholic symbol system or the Catholic experience that holds an answer to the social questions phrased above?

To answer that, we must further clarify the Catholic view of the nature of human nature. Insofar as I understand the position, Catholics must take a stand for maximizing the opportunities for individual choice. A virtuous society, in other words, is created not by imposing detailed and precise legal regulations on every aspect of human behavior but by maximizing freedom and responsibility within broad structures where people are free enough and secure enough to have no especially powerful motivation for not acting generously or virtuously. As one theologian put it to me (departing considerably from his Protestant tradition), "Humankind is good unless it is frightened."

A Catholic contribution to social policy would be to insist that in a just society no individual or group would be so frightened that its fundamental self-interests were endangered to the extent that it had to strike back or strike out before it was struck down. To put the matter somewhat differently, a Catholic contribution to social policy would emphasize the need for reconciliation and coalition building, for creating social policies with which everyone can live, and for building into social policies absolute guarantees that the basic self-interests of a group would not be threatened.

It ought to be relatively easy, for example, to institute a program of integration insurance. Large numbers of people (the majority of the population) have no objection to living in integrated neighborhoods, particularly if the crime rate can be controlled. But many people are afraid, and quite properly, that racial integration means a temporary collapse of home values and the real possibility that they will suffer severe financial losses. The fear, of course, becomes a self-fulfilling prophecy precisely because the tendency to sell out before the market value is depressed leads only to rapid depression throughout the neighborhood. If there were some sort of insurance to guarantee a homeowner the equity in his house when racial integration occurs, then blockbusting, panic peddling, and rapid neighborhood turnover would be drastically curtailed if not eliminated. Racial integration, then, would not be merely a brief interlude between white to black ghettoization.

Why hasn't such a simple social intervention been attempted? I would suggest that the reason is that a completely different perspective on urban social policy exists among the intellectual and journalist elites. The city is divided into the "good" groups and the "bad" groups, or, if you will, the "oppressed" groups and the "oppressor" groups. The good groups are the blacks, the Spanish-speaking, and the American Indians; the bad are the ethnics—the Poles, the Italians, the Lithuanians, the Hungarians, the Irish, and the lower-middle-class and working-class Jews. In between the good and the bad groups are the cultural elites—mostly Protestant, upper-middle-class Jewish, and a few Irish Catholic renegades. It is up to these groups to take from the oppressor and give to the oppressed. The home values go down in Polish neighborhoods, but it serves them right because they are, after all, racists. On the other hand, public housing is often imposed on urban neighborhoods by lawyers and judges who live in suburbia, but would not impose public housing on their own suburbs.

Still another contribution of the Catholic perspective to social policy discussion might be an insistence on the importance of family and local community. Social policy makers, with some exceptions, are intellectuals. That means they have the intellectual's passion for neatness, order, and elegance. Unfortunately, the human population of the country is patterned geographically, culturally, and psychologically in ways that are not neat and elegant. So rambling, ramshackle neighborhoods with crooked streets must be torn down to be replaced by giant skyscrapers or expressways; city or regionwide programs which look beautiful on organization charts must be imposed even if the little strong and vital nooks and crannies of a city's communities are snuffed out. Similarly, family structure that may vary from the upper-middle-class, quasi-liberated family is thought to be regressive. The traditional family structures of the ethnic groups (and here I would certainly include the traditional black and Spanish-speaking families) are viewed as an obstacle to social progress or at least as irrelevant to social policy considerations.

Social policy, if it is to make any sense at all, must take into account the considerable heterogeneity of family structures, role expectations, and values concerning intimate behavior that can be found among the diverse communities that constitute our society. In other words, both on the subject of family and on the subject of local community, a Catholic contribution to social policy would be to argue for the importance of sensitivity to grass roots independence, diversity, and responsibility. You can rub out the neighborhood, you can ignore it, you can turn it over to social workers; or you can coop-

erate with it, understand it, strike a bargain with it, integrate it into
your coalition. Of course, the skills required to do it are more likely
to be found in a ward commissioner with a high school education
than in an OEO administrator with a Ph.D.

My friend Ralph Whitehead had some trenchant thoughts on the
Catholic communal ethic vis à vis the therapeutic ethic. He wrote in a
letter to me:

The communal sense can then begin to ask some questions of the
therapeutic ethic, or put it through some paces. For one thing, we can
ask, how well does the therapeutic ethic travel *outside* the clinical
setting where it arose? Surely the relationship of government, policy
and the citizen cannot, perhaps even symbolically, let alone literally,
approximate or even parallel the relationship of psychiatric social
worker to the individual client. The therapeutic social policy must be
translated into a legal brief, thence into a court ruling, thence into
departmental policy, thence into guidelines, thence into memoranda
of intent . . .; and by the time it shows up on 79th Street, it is quite a
different creature. Thus, this model must bend to bureaucratic
realities, political realities. . . . It's one thing to add an option for
schooling or work—the estimable and reasonable goal of some
policies—and something else completely to expect or assume a
transformation of identity, personality. Put differently, I can readily
understand a business agent for the plumbers saying to the therapist:
"A few months ago this kid was going to destroy all of America's
institutions. Today, I'm supposed to send him out on a job for $8.80
an hour. Isn't there a chance he might act up?"

He puts it still more simply, "Or as the precinct captain, animated
by the communal sense of human nature might reply to the therapeutic reformer, 'Fine, but how're you going to *organize* all this?' "

Whitehead discusses further the "precinct ethos":

If people find explications of the precinct ethos to be laughable, they
ought to be made to confront some functional equivalencies. For instance, the history of more than fifteen years of one strain of urban

social reform—going back to Mobilization for Youth—could be read as an attempt by well-meaning Jewish practitioners to turn public schools used by blacks and Latins into focal institutions for communal life, that is, into parish schools. This strain would carry us through Ocean Hill, I'd claim. The public schools did well by their Jewish pupils for a variety of reasons, including many I wouldn't understand. Thus, given this faith, and unmindful of how particularistic it was, Jewish reformers, obviously and fairly encouraged by the pervasiveness of public education (gauged by legal sanctions, dollars spent, numbers enrolled, hours occupied, etc.—its impact enormous) tried to use it as a base to fashion the parish and the political clubhouse. Yet, as far as I've been able to determine by considerable reading, these planners and reformers never looked to experience for any guidance—and they've failed accordingly. Our tradition is persistently shunted aside by a scholarly phrase, "after the fall of the big-city machines . . . " or else it is ignored altogether or at least rarely viewed as it is: the longest and strongest and broadest tradition of settlement house work in this country provided simply enough by the rectory and the convent. But just try to tell it to a professor of social welfare.

Precisely because it takes for granted the complexity and diversity of the world in which everyday life is lived, the Catholic ethic has a far more realistic (rather than theoretical) skepticism than either the utilitarian or therapeutic ethics. It is skeptical about the potentiality for success in any given plan or program. It is remarkably clear eyed about the messiness of all things human; it expects no great success, nor is it dismayed by failure. It does not normally swing from great, enthusiastic highs to deep, depressed lows, as did, for example, Protestant theology in the late 1960s when it swung from the enthusiastic Harvey Cox's *Secular City* to the apocalyptic despair of some of the ecological theologians.

The Catholic ethic is far more benign about both humankind and human society but far more skeptical about plans to improve both. Perhaps the explanation for this paradox is that if you assume the fundamental goodness of humankind you are able to be more tolerant of its accidental imperfections even when such imperfections seem monumental. You want to see social change and progress, of course, but because you are more hopeful in the long run, you are able to be realistic about failure in the short. Such a world view generates less passionate righteousness, perhaps, but also less passionate self-righteousness.

The American Catholic ethic, paradoxically, is grounded in the American historical experience. The left-right framework of issue oriented politics has been imposed on us by our intellectuals and journalists who feel that since that is the way European politics operates, that's the way any politics ought to operate. But the fundamental experience of American political life was shaped not by a revolution against an established church and aristocracy and a hereditary monarchy but rather by the phenomena of integration, westward migration, and the Civil War. The left-right issue politics may make sense in those societies where there was a 1789, an 1848, and an 1870, but the Civil War split the country into North and South, the immigration of the Catholic ethnic groups split the country into Catholic urbanite and rural Protestant, and the westward migration produced populism and progressivism; and this constitutes the matrix for American political life. American politics is much less about issues than it is about groups struggling for their place in the political and social sun. Since no group is a majority in American society, American politics is necessarily coalition politics, the politics of winning allies, obtaining consensus, working compromises. This is, of course, precisely what James Madison had in mind.

The ultimate crucible of coalition politics is the precinct, the grass roots political unit whose importance has been belatedly recognized by even the independents and the reformers. People vote, quite literally, where they live.

However much its theorists may have overlooked the fact, the American Catholic church in practice has been fully aware of pluralism. How can you avoid being aware of it when you are made up of Irish, Italians, Poles, Lithuanians, Czechs, Ukranians, Slovaks, Slovenes, etc., etc.?

You take the parish and you add to it the precinct and you get that most unique American Catholic phenomenon, the neighborhood. I have always been amused by the enthusiasm with which priest and religious discuss the "building of community," forgetting that in the neighborhood one has the most astonishing and incredible manifestation of community in the whole urban industrial world. Because we all came from neighborhoods and took them for granted we never realized how special they were until finally, and foolishly, we began to eliminate them. We search in vain in the Catholic intellectual and literary efforts of the last several decades for even the slightest awareness of the existence of the neighborhood. Not only were neighborhoods not worth understanding, they were not even worth criticizing. There is some neighborhood sense in James Farrell's *Studs Lonigan,* but between *Studs Lonigan* and the 1974 film, *Mean Streets,* one can find little about neighborhoods.

It is interesting that several non-Catholic observers, such as Robert Schrank, are insisting on the importance of the Catholic contribution to social policy formation. A number of younger Catholics, too, such as Philip Murnion, Geno Baroni, Paul Asciolla, Ralph Whitehead, Michael Novak, James Barry, William McCready and Pastora San Juan Cafferty, are groping towards an articulation of a social policy and a social ethic founded in the Catholic world view and the Catholic experience. In a decisive article on the "neighborhood ethic," McCready summarizes that ethic in the "Polish proverb" seen on a precinct captain's desk: "Goya/kod." The "proverb" is in fact an anachronym for "get off your ass, knock on doors." Such is the Catholic ethic!

Still, this group is dissident as far as the mainstream of Catholic beliefs is concerned. This is evidenced by the ceaseless pounding that Michael Novak takes from official Catholic liberals, and by the intense popularity of liberation theology in the Catholic community long after our Protestant brothers began rapidly to distance themselves from its bizarre jerry-built structure.

Latin American theologizing has replaced German, French, and Dutch as the new conventional wisdom of the American Catholic elite. Priests, nuns, seminarians, young lay people parrot its cliches.

One cannot have a meeting of major superiors without someone arriving on the scene with the newest wisdoms from the third world; and at institutes up and down the length and breadth of the land each summer, hard working priests and religious hear socialist critiques of everything they do and everything they stand for. They dutifully copy these critiques in their notebooks and go home, with increased guilt feelings, to do exactly what they have been doing all along, because liberation theology, however passionate, is quite irrelevant to the American environment. The enthusiasm of the Catholic elites for it, as Geno Baroni notes, is a sign that the elites are on the verge of cultural bankruptcy. Indeed they are.

It may be that liberation theology has some pertinence in Latin America, though I doubt it. A more dispassionate view, recently expressed by Robert Heilbroner, is that the so-called emerging nations need extremely strong governments instead of "liberation" to force the necessary discipline and change on reluctant social structures and cultures that will be required if these nations are to cope with their populations and modernization problems. It may not matter whether a nation has a right-wing dictatorship, as in Brazil, a left-wing dictatorship, as in Peru, or a Marxist police state, as in Cuba. A nation does not need liberation but a strong governmental hand. In any case, the liberation theologians haven't liberated anybody, and they are not likely to do so. They reflect theologically on what they have not done, and the poor, self-hating North American Catholics are incapable of reflecting theologically on what they have done.

People laugh—when they don't jeer—when I raise the possibility of a "theology of the precinct." What I mean, of course, is that Catholics need to reflect theologically on the American Catholic experience both as part of a painful process of self-understanding and as a prelude to making their own unique contribution to American society, to the church universal, and to humankind. They shall never so reflect as long as they are content with the warmed-over efforts of people from other lands. In fact, the precinct, the parish, the neighborhood are the places where reconciliation has occurred. There is, of course, not nearly as much racial, religious, and ethnic harmony in American society as there ought to be. Yet, when the model for comparison is not what ought to be but what exists in other parts of the world, then what has occurred in the precincts and the wards of the big cities looks impressive. Surely there is some sort of reconciliation indicated by the one third of the Catholics who live in integrated neighborhoods in the country and the two thirds of the Catholic school children who go to integrated schools.

The social policy of the country and the cultural elites is still vigorously if not altogether consciously anti-Catholic. "Communalism," "ethnicity," "particularism" are all bad things, and the Catholic ethic is reactionary by definition. It was thought that with the Vatican Council Catholics would change, but after a burst of ecumenical enthusiasm it has become clear that the Catholic populace has not changed, however much some Catholics paid the price of alienation in their attempt to become accepted by the cultural and social policy elites of the country. It was no accident that at the "New Class" Democratic convention of 1972, it was precisely the Catholic Daley and the Catholic Meany who were tossed out on their ears. Further, the Catholic ethnics are viewed as the principal obstacles to enlightened social change. Some people may believe that a uniquely important contribution can come out of the Catholic neighborhoods, precincts, parishes, union locals, and schools; but most American social policy and cultural elites find the notion absurd if not odious (to use the favorite word of the *Village Voice*).

And the so-called Catholic intelligentsia, who still want so desperately to belong, goes along beating its collective breast or alternately citing meaningless quotations (with or without translation) from Paulo Friere or Gustavo Gutierez. It may take another generation before either Catholics or non-Catholics are willing to take seriously a reflection on the meaning of the American Catholic experience, much less to consider how the Catholic ethic has reshaped (and been reshaped in) the crucible of American urban pluralism.

By that time all the precinct captains will be dead.

CHAPTER EIGHT

The Experience
of the Neighborhood

One thing the communal Catholic knows: neighborhoods are good places. He has fond memories of the old neighborhood in which he grew up and wishes that his children might grow up in a modernized version of the "old neighborhood." Often, he chooses his place to live because it looks like it might be a neighborhood; and, almost without knowing it, he sets about building up a neighborhood spirit almost as soon as he has moved into it.

He is therefore part of the dissenting minority of Americans with his educational attainment. Social reformers and high-level do-gooders view neighborhoods as at best irrelevant and at worst an obstacle. The best thing you can do to a neighborhood is obliterate it with a bulldozer and put up an expressway or a high rise housing project.

And the romantic Catholic elites are not romantic about neighborhoods. On the contrary, they hate them; having rejected their own past, they must do all that they can to deny that past to others. The old neighborhood must be ridiculed and denounced; or alternatively, it is praised, but then written off as a relic of the past which is irrelevant to the present.

Baloney . . .

Sociologists have a hard time defining a neighborhood. Herbert

Gans, using the cultural approach, calls it "the urban village."
Gerald Suttles, from the social psychological perspective, maintains
that the neighborhood by definition is a place to be defended. It is
that segment of the checkerboard of the city in which one feels safe.
Demographers try to define it in socioeconomic terms. The United
States Census thinks of the neighborhood as a census tract. Some researchers try to define a neighborhood empirically, in terms of the
praxis, the "practical experience" of neighbors.

Unfortunately, the subjective definitions of neighborhood give rise
to several different opinions of what the boundaries of the neighborhood are. Furthermore, the neighborhood exists on several different
levels. The block on which one's neighbors live (across the alley in
many of the "old" neighborhoods, across the street in many of the
"new" ones), the one or two blocks surrounding one's own where it
is considered "safe" for younger children to play, and the "broader
community" from which the neighborhood may get its name and
wider identification are all proper uses of the term "neighborhood."
In the south side of Chicago, for example, the neighborhood may be
for all practical purposes coterminous with the parish. Thus, young
people when asked where they are from would not say "Brainard" or
"Englewood" or "Beverly" but "St. Killians," "St. Leo," "St.
Barnabas." Even Protestants seem to get into the habit of identifying
their neighborhoods by the name of the Catholic parish not so much
out of ecumenical motives but simply, one supposes, for clarity of
discourse. Some neighborhoods are large enough to have several
parishes, and in old neighborhoods with national parishes, many
shared the same territory.

The people who use the neighborhood know what it is, and they
know what the word "neighborhood" means. The social scientist
who hears them must be careful to understand in which sense the
word is being used. Its ambiguity does not mean that the reality does
not exist, as some social scientists have argued, but that the reality is
multiple. Language is not designed for the precision of sociological
analysis; it reflects, rather, the complexity of social reality.

It is not clear to me whether cities other than American have neighborhoods, or even whether all American cities have them.* Insofar as I can tell, the boroughs of London, the arrondissements of Paris, the districts of Rome, Vienna, and Berlin are not neighborhoods in the sense the word has acquired in the south side of Chicago, Brooklyn, Boston, Detroit, St. Louis, Milwaukee, and the other cities of the northeast and north central regions of the United States. However, James Duran describes the creation of enclaves in a city in Kenya in which tribes become ethnic groups. Duran's ethnic enclaves sound suspiciously like neighborhoods. Perhaps "foreign" immigration of diverse tribes is required for the neighborhood, in the American sense at least, to come into being.

Neighborhoods may well have existed in Paris and London in the nineteenth century, but the country folk flocking to those two cities were, after all, English and French; they never became ethnic groups as did the immigrants to American cities, and, it would seem, to Duran's Kenyan city. London would make an interesting case study. In addition to the official map provided by the boroughs, there surely is in modern London an unofficial map marking out the boundaries of the various ethnic enclaves in that multiracial, multiethnic polyglot city. I have the impression that there are indeed neighborhoods in London, though perhaps they are not as clearly defined or as important for self-identity as their counterparts in the United States.

Although neighborhoods in the northeast and north central parts of the United States were the crucible of the immigrants' experience, we have very little history of that immigrant experience. As Jay Dolan remarks in his Ph.D. dissertation, "For many years American Catholic historiography has focused on episcopal biographies and the internal controversies of the church in the late nineteenth century. As a result there has been little writing done on the urban dimension of

*I have heard it argued that Los Angeles is devoid of neighborhoods. Such may well be true of the vast tract developments of the San Rafael and San Fernando Valleys; it may also be true, for all I know, of Orange County; it is surely not true of the city of Los Angeles itself.

the American Catholic church."* The historiography of which Dolan
writes is relatively unconcerned with the social dimensions of history
and is quite out of touch with the mainstream of recent American historical thought. It is no discredit to Thomas McAvoy or John Tracy
Ellis to say that the work they and their students have done represents
a much earlier phase of American historiography, a phase in which
facts and events are narrated with little attention paid to social or
economic context. General theoretical models like "Americanization" or "the influence of the frontier" may be added to the narrative
descriptions of the institutional histories and biographies but scarcely
flow from the data or admit testing or further research. In fact, as
Dolan points out, it is not the frontier but the city, not Americanization but cultural pluralism that is the distinctive phenomenon of the
American Catholic experience. In his study of the development of
the Catholic neighborhoods and parishes in New York City from the
early to middle nineteenth century, Dolan establishes conclusively
that the emergence of the national parish (there were none in New
York in 1815; by 1865, they constituted one third of the parishes in
the diocese) was the unique adaptation of Catholicism to the
pluralism of American cities.

    Dolan writes:

In studying American Catholicism from an urban perspective the
similar characteristics of different urban churches are strikingly exhi-
bited. The unity of American Catholicism is thus more readily perceived and when combined with the cultural pluralism of its people,
the genius of American Catholicism becomes more evident. Briefly
stated, this genius may be described as unity in the midst of cultural
pluralism. The unity is based on a common faith, a common church
and a common country, and the unifying effect of the urban environment should not be underestimated. In each urban church there

---

*Jay P. Dolan, "Urban Catholicism: New York City 1815–1897." Unpublished
Ph.D. dissertation, University of Chicago, 1970, p. iii.

were common problems, similar national groupings, and similar patterns of organization together with similar educational and benevolent apostolates. Such similarities naturally linked the church in Chicago with the church in New York and in other large cities and this communality helped to shape the self identity of American Catholicism. The identity began to take shape during the middle decades of the nineteenth century when urbanization in America proceeded at a rate faster than ever before.*

It was Archbishop John Hughes who recognized that nationalism was "an exceedingly tender and delicate topic." Dolan comments:

In encouraging the organization of national parishes in the city and the diocese, he lessened the possibilities of conflict and recognized the inherent differences between ethnic groups. During the middle decades of the century the national parish became the church's adaptation to the variety of people living in the city and as the immigrants continued to swell the urban population later in the century the national parish became even more necessary. When the church ignored the ethnicity of its people and failed to recruit ethnic priests and to establish national parishes, then conflict inevitably arose.†

But despite the national parish and the potential for disunity it involved, there were still the unifying factors of commitment to American society and its precious gift of freedom. Dolan notes:

Appealing to their adopted patriotism, Catholic spokesmen quickly acquired the style of a Fourth of July orator. The public exhibitions of parochial school students encouraged patriotic poems and songs; and the two great principles which guided the New York Catholic paper, *Freeman's Journal*, were to be truly Catholic and truly American.‡

*Ibid., p. 288.

† Ibid., p. 294.

‡Ibid., p. 294.

Characteristic of the American national parish was the organizational control exercised by the chancery office. Dolan implies that the reasons American bishops seemed to have so much more power vis à vis their priests than do bishops in other parts of the world is that a highly centralized diocesan administration was a sine qua non for holding together the diversity of their very pluralistic dioceses.

It must be remembered that the church leadership had to contend with immigrants not only from diverse countries, but from diverse social structures. They not only had a religion, they had a role. The priest or the pastor came very early; so, too, I suspect, did the tavern owner and the shopkeeper; and not too long after, the undertaker and the political leader arrived. The earlier groups did not bring professionals with them, save for an occasional doctor perhaps. Yet it would not take long for a young man of seventeen, if he was bright and ambitious, to find his way to medical school or law school and begin professional practice in the neighborhood. Orders of teaching nuns, perhaps from the old country or, as in some cases, founded in the United States to recruit people from the old country, would begin the parochial school. Young women from the community would go to "normal" schools and take up jobs teaching in the public schools, if not in their own neighborhoods nearby.

The speed with which the community neighborhood developed its own services must have varied from group to group and have been closely connected with which of the group's members could acquire the English language. One can today go into one of the older ethnic neighborhoods of a city and see the social structure of the immigrant neighborhood. For example, on South Lowe in Chicago (Mayor Daley's street, which ought to be preserved as a national monument) one can find within one block the police station, the fire station, the Catholic church, the politician's house (in this case, a very important man), the undertaker's, the corner grocery store, and the tavern. In newer neighborhoods the tavern may be replaced by the country club and the corner grocery by the supermarket, but the other institutions have survived.

The parish developed within this service community, protecting the religious faith of the people even on those occasions when the faithful didn't want protection. It also frequently provided for the people's material welfare and promoted their political advance.

The neighborhood was also the educational base, particularly in the parochial school. In some communities, Catholics so dominated the public school system that it was scarcely necessary to build a parochial school (particularly in the Boston area). In Holy Family parish on the west side of Chicago in the years between the Civil War and the Great Chicago Fire, the legendary Father Damen (after whom Damen Avenue in Chicago is named) had five schools within his parish boundaries, including one "college," a four-year preparatory and two-year collegiate institution which eventually grew to be Loyola University. The immigrants learned quickly that education was the way to make it in American society. To send their children to secondary school and then in the next generation into higher education became the dream of every parent.

It is of critical importance to realize that there was almost no such thing as a homogenous ethnic neighborhood, not at least after the Civil War. One can stand in the Bridgeport section of Chicago and see within three blocks five church steeples—the Polish, the Czech, the German, the Lithuanian, and the Irish. The Irish church was a territorial parish which has more recently become known as the Italian parish. All Saints, St. John Nepomucene, St. Anthony, St. Barbara, all represented different ethnic enclaves within the same neighborhood. (On one street corner in the city of Rome, New York, there are four different churches and a fifth a half block away.) Even neighborhoods where the density of national churches was not so great almost always had at least two and usually more ethnic groups cooperating, competing, struggling, getting along.

From the beginning the neighborhood had to absorb diversity, the diversity of the Old World and the new, of the recent immigrants (the "greenhorns"), and the old timers, and finally the diversity of styles, religion, and customs within the ethnic collectivities themselves. The single-group ethnic neighborhood is mostly a myth, though there were certainly areas of the city where one group was more concentrated and dominant than others. If one looks at census material even in the years around the turn of the century, one will find few homogenous neighborhoods. If the neighborhood was not ethnically diverse from the beginning, it soon became so. The near west side of Chicago, for example, was "Little Italy" and also "Greektown." The Irish had to share the south side of Chicago with Germans and Swedes, and later Italians, Poles, Lithuanians, and blacks. There was not always peace and fraternity among these diverse groups; the tragic 1919 race riot was somber evidence that pluralism didn't always work. Perhaps the amazing thing, though, is that there were so few racial and ethnic riots in the big cities after 1870.

Were the neighborhoods good places to live? Most of those who lived in them thought so, and still think so. In the Taylor Street and Bridgeport neighborhood of Chicago, for example, many people could easily move to more affluent communities but will not do so because of the depth of their affection for the neighborhood. Those of us who may be two or three generations removed from the immigrant experience but who have still lived and worked in neighborhoods are perfectly willing to testify that they can be warm, supportive places. A good neighborhood becomes part of your life; you can never really leave it behind. Even in the 1970s many young people decide to move back to their neighborhoods if they can. A neighborhood is something less than an extended family, but it is something infinitely more than an undifferentiated suburban housing tract.*

But the neighborhood has gotten a bad press from those Catholic intellectuals who left it—usually feeling they were driven out. If one reads James Farrell's *Studs Lonigan,* then one need not bother with any attacks by lesser writers on the narrow, wretched parochialism of the neighborhood, a place of "spiritual poverty," as Farrell puts it.

---

*The children of one of my NORC colleagues are the fourth generation of his family to live in the same neighborhood. One quarter of the American Catholic population live either in the neighborhood in which they grew up or close to it.

Of course the intellectual perforce had to question the institutions of the neighborhood. Unless he was an extraordinarily well balanced and mature person, he had to fight the neighborhood and flee from it eventually if he was to pursue his intellectual vocation. However, my impression is that by the 1930s, and certainly by the 1940s, the situation had changed considerably. Intellectuals still left, but more, I think, to work out their own psychological problems than because the neighborhood would not tolerate them. By the 1950s, neighborhoods became quite proud of the Ph.D.'s, college professors, writers, and artists that they might find living on their streets.

No one need tell me that neighborhoods are parochial, that they can be narrow, dull, rigid, inflexible, intolerant places.* If you are going to have *gemeinschaft* in the midst of a *gesellschaft* world, I can see no way for you to avoid narrowness and parochialism. The new counterculture communes seem little different from the old neighborhoods in this respect. Nor need anyone tell me that in their South Side bastions the Chicago Irish can be suspicious, rigid, narrow people. I suspect I know this far better than any of the authors who prattle glibly about "ghetto Catholicism." However, I have also been on the margins of the intellectual and academic community. I have lived in Hyde Park, Chicago, which can be characterized fairly as a Jewish intellectual neighborhood. In its own way, Hyde Park is as parochial as Beverly; and in their own way, the Jewish intellegentsia are as narrow as the Irish lawyer-politicians. Humankind tends to be parochial, in other words, and the old neighborhoods are not much different from the university communities in this respect.

I would still argue that neighborhoods are incredibly diversified places. They are more diversified than the one-class professional

*My downfall in a neighborhood in which I worked as a priest began when I started to write books. The people in the community were convinced that my books were about them and that I said terrible things about them. "Everyone knew" what I was writing, of course, though few people ever read the books, and what was in them really supported their side. I was never against them. I am reminded of G. K. Chesterton's book, *Orthodoxy,* which was banned in Russia because the censors assumed that it was about Russian orthodoxy and therefore to be banned.

suburbs, and more diversified than the one-occupation university communities. The neighborhood was and is the microcosm of pluralism. The young, the middle-aged, and the old; the toddler, the school child, the teen-ager, the young unmarried, the just-married, the parents, and the aged matriarchs and patriarchs of the family all live there. In the neighborhood most people are Democrats, but there are Republicans, too, complete with their own precinct captains and ward committeemen. A few in the neighborhood are very rich or very poor, but most neighborhoods have been both blue collar and white collar, both college-trained professional and manual worker. Some people worked in the neighborhood, some not; some ran their own business, some worked for large companies. Some lived their lives for their children, others expected the children to live their lives for their parents. While there were very few radicals and perhaps a few more reactionaries, there was still a wide range of political opinion in the neighborhood; no one was under moral constraint to repeat a fashionable party line.

The neighborhood had room for cranks and crabs, for the physically and mentally handicapped. Every real neighborhood, as a matter of fact, has to have at least one crank (the man who raises guinea pigs in his garage), one crab (he calls the police every time kids go by his house), and one or more haunted houses. You can put the matter another way. If there is no haunted house, you haven't got a neighborhood. Mr. Ed the Weatherman (he remembers what the weather was every day of the past forty years), Sam Sam the Candyman (he gives candy to all the kids on the street), and the Cat Lady (she lives in a twisted, unpainted house with a vast number of felines) are more than just neighborhood characters; they are evidence that the neighborhood is strong enough in its patterned relationships, its customs, and folkways to tolerate not only diversity but some eccentricity and a pinch of the bizarre.

If you want privacy in the neighborhood you can have it; if you want community, you can have that too. One young man who lived in an upper-middle-class Irish neighborhood told me that for three weeks after his wife was suddenly hospitalized with an almost fatal illness, he came home from work to discover a different neighbor preparing the family supper every night. *Gemeinschaft* like this is hard to come by. Still, if you want to be a recluse, that's all right too. The kids may make up stories about you, but if you are determined in your reclusivity, you won't give a damn what they say anyhow.

The neighborhood also generates tremendous loyalty. If you encounter someone from your neighborhood halfway around the world, or if you receive a letter from someone you knew in the neighborhood thirty years ago, there is a compulsion to respond as though he were a close friend whether the relationship within the neighborhood was particularly friendly or not. Neighborhood people are special. You feel a certain obligation to them and they to you. It is easy to see in this mutuality of obligation a continuation in the urban environment of the old peasant loyalties of village and clan. Surely the loyalties a neighborhood generates are less formalized and less ritualized than those to an extended family in a farming community in the west of Ireland, let us say. In a way, however, the neighborhood ties can be even more powerful because they are to some extent a matter of free choice.

Of critical importance to the neighborhood are the places where people can gather. The front porch or the door stoop is the primary gathering place. The absence of both these structures in the suburbs may be one of the reasons why communal life deteriorates so quickly there. I simply cannot believe that something as important to American society for generations as the front porch was eliminated without resistance in almost all construction since 1945. Another important institution which is rare in the suburbs is the alley. It was only secondarily a place for garbage trucks, primarily a communication channel for neighboring. For reasons not altogether clear to me, an alley linked people together rather than separating them. In the neighborhood you were close to the people who lived across the alley from you, even closer to them than those who lived across the street. In the suburbs, however, you interact with the people across the street. Perhaps all this has to do with the location of parking lots and garbage cans.

The secondary meeting places in the neighborhood were the candy store, the drugstore corner, the pool hall, and the tavern. Most of these have been eliminated from the suburbs. In Beverly, where I lived for ten years, the drugstore corner was there, but many of the quasi-suburbanite adults who lived in Beverly felt that adolescents "hanging around" that corner were an abomination. They did everything they could to destroy the institution. Unfortunately, they were successful. In many Catholic parishes—where the pastor's disposition permits—schoolyards make a good place for "hanging around." In the occasional extraordinary parish, the rectory basement serves that purpose admirably.

The clean, neat, antiseptic suburbs, laid out by city planners or built haphazardly by developers, may have all kinds of parks and educational facilities, but they rarely provide young people with any place to "hang out." Small wonder they take to hot rods and drugs. The point is that the front porch, the door stoop, the drugstore corner, and the alley were all institutions that contributed to the toleration of, if not the reinforcement of, diversity. Their disappearance was a strong factor making for homogeneity.

The current nostalgia for the past has temporarily reversed the literary distaste for the neighborhood. The brilliant film *Mean Streets* signals the turn. The New York hero argues repeatedly with the young loan shark that he cannot charge exorbitant interest rates to "somebody from the neighborhood." His own concern about his half-mad friend is based in substantial part on the fact that the friend is "from the neighborhood." In a peasant society obligations to one's "connections" are clear and specific; in a neighborhood they tend to be much more diffuse. And this is precisely the problem the hero of *Mean Streets* has: he can't tell where his obligations to his friend end, and hence finds himself caught in tragedy. It is a brilliant portrait of the kaleidoscopic variety and the immense social power as well as the profound emotional intensity that marks life in a neighborhood. Clearly the director of *Mean Streets* feels ambivalent about his neighborhood. But that is progress. For Jimmy Farrell there was no ambivalence at all, only hatred. Many who have seen *Mean*

Streets do not find its neighborhood attractive. The movie is surely a portrayal of the dark side of neighborhood life, but it is nonetheless a superb presentation of the raw, elemental strength that vibrates through neighborhood life. The argument of the present chapter is that one of the things neighborhoods are good for is to tolerate variety and diversity, The Christ-haunted hero of *Mean Streets,* his epileptic girlfriend, her half-mad cousin, the loan shark, and the mafia don are all testimony to that variety.

Rosabeth Moss Kanter, a sociologist at Brandeis University, has written in *Working Papers* a superb article on urban communes. Ms. Kanter concedes that most urban communes have a very short life, but she argues that they are still important because they represent a trend in the larger society toward relationships that are not stereotyped by age and sex. I wonder. Writing a century ago about communards, Horace Greeley (no relation) commented, "the conceited, the crotchety, the selfish, the headstrong, the pugnacious, the unappreciated, the played-out, the idle, the good-for-nothing, generally, who finding themselves utterly out of place or at discount in the world as it is, rashly concluded that they were exactly fitted for the world as it should be." One might well say the same thing about the present generation of communards.

There is less age and sex stereotyping in the neighborhood than there is in the one-class, one-age suburb. While the neighborhood has standards about appropriate behavior for people of various ages of both sexes, there is a wide latitude in the application of these standards, precisely because most neighborhoods contain different generations and different occupational groupings. In the neighborhood, for example, a woman may work if she wants to, and in the lower-middle-class and working-class neighborhoods women have had jobs—if not careers—for a long time without ever needing a "liberation movement" to legitimate such occupations. But a woman can also be "just a housewife" if she wants, an option scarcely left any more to a woman in a university community. Nor is there anything in the neighborhood nearly so rigid as the status structure imposed on the university community by the tenure and promotion system or, in a one-class suburb, by salary, automobiles, fur coats, and foreign vacations. In the neighborhoods I know best, the people with the most money by no means have the highest status, and the highest status people are not necessarily wealthy.

I do not wish to idealize or romanticize the neighborhood. More than most of its critics I know what its weaknesses are. I would still contend that the neighborhood has had considerable success in three main enterprises:

1. Facilitating the transition from the Old World to the new, and the later transition from the working class to the middle class.

2. Creating in the midst of industrial urban society a community with immense social and emotional strength.

3. Tolerating within its boundaries more age, class, occupational, and attitudinal diversity than is to be found either in the new suburbs or in intellectual communities.

I take it that the first two points are scarcely arguable. Many read ers will be offended by the third. I would merely suggest that they take a closer look to see if they have not confused verbal sophistication with diversity.

I have distinguished between neighborhoods—"old," toward the center city, and "new," toward its fringes—and the suburbs. There is a considerable difference of opinion as to whether neighborhoods appear in upper-middle-class suburbs. Most Catholic observers contend that the suburbs are without neighborhoods. But Beverly, the neighborhood I knew best, was a strange combination of city and suburb. Suburban in its income and life-style, urban in its legal status and in its political involvement, it surely proved that neighborhood community was not at all incompatible with high mean income and education. It would have been hard to think of a neighborhood more intensely communitarian than Beverly.

Both literature and social science have paid relatively little attention to what I think is one of the most extraordinary phenomena of American urban life. Indeed, I have heard people say in the skyscrapers of midtown Manhattan, "In New York City we don't have neighborhoods." All they had to do is go to the window, look across the East River to find neighborhoods aplenty. In fact, they drive through one of the great neighborhoods, Astoria, on their way to LaGuardia Airport, and they probably never even notice it.

The old "Chicago school" of sociology was fascinated by neighborhoods, but sometime in the middle 1930s to 1940s, the Chicago school ran out of steam. Attempts to revive it have produced nothing but Suttles' brilliant work (and he is no longer at the University of Chicago). Of course, neighborhood life does not admit of analysis in mathematical models, which is the current mainstream of sociological research. There has been a revival of "participant observation" in sociology in recent years, but the new generation of such observers are "socially committed" and usually "radical," which means they would hardly be interested in neighborhoods of white people.*

And since the neighborhood is an especially if not uniquely Catholic creation, Catholics more than others could be expected to have an interest in studying the social structure of neighborhoods and reflecting on the religious meaning of the neighborhood phenomenon. That they have not done so is simply one more bit of evidence of the appalling lack of self-awareness in American Catholicism. They have ignored the symbol that, to use the Tillichian term, "correlates" with the praxis of neighborhood life, with the ministry of the church to the neighborhood community. That symbol is *the church,* the assembly of God's people, the multifunctioned body of Christ.

The church correlates with the neighborhood precisely insofar as the church is catholic with a small "c." You put up with the shanty Irishmen or the suspicious Polacks or the dumb Germans or the hot-tempered dagos precisely because, damn it all, it was their church as much as it was yours. And the marvelous quotation from *Finnegans Wake* says it all: "Catholicism means, here comes everybody." And that includes the local idiot, those awful people down by the tracks, the corrupt politician, the priest who drinks too much, the Italians

---

*Having lived in black neighborhoods for ten years, I am struck with how quickly an immigrating black population reconstructs a neighborhood structure that is very like the white structure it has replaced.

who, as my mother used to say when I was growing up on the west side of Chicago, "bring noise into the neighborhood with them." The unique and most fundamental insight of Catholic Christianity is that the net must be thrown very far and very wide indeed. Catholicism, in other words, does not see the need to homogenize. The richness and variety of the neighborhood reflect the richness and variety of God's people. In another chapter, I quote John Higham as observing that America's "pluralistic integration" reflects a tolerance for a society whose divisions are vague and whose boundaries are "messy." Neighborhoods are vague and messy places precisely because if you try to draw neat, sharp lines in neighborhoods you end up with nothing left. He who presides over a neighborhood does not try to eliminate its diversity; if he does the neighborhood will flow like water through his fingers, like sand through a sieve. Rather he respects its richness and diversity, tolerates and even enjoys its messiness, and attempts to reconcile on a day-to-day practical basis the diverse peoples who live there.

The ultimate lesson, then, of the praxis of the ministry of the church in the neighborhood is that reconciliation is never neat, never permanent, never clear or sharp. It is a messy, ambiguous, uncertain, transient business never done with once and for all but begun anew each day.

The reconciler, the one who convenes the body of the people and presides over the endless ebb and flow of the people's interaction, is a pragmatic, sensitive person able to tolerate ambiguity and possessing a "feel" for the subtle dynamics of changing human relationships. You don't do your reconciliation in the office or the rectory; you do it in the back of the church on Sunday mornings, walking the streets of the parish on a late autumn afternoon, and maybe just hanging around.

The praxis of the parish reveals the human condition in all its complex, ambiguous, uncertain, messy dynamics. It suggests that the church is best built up, reconstructed, and reinforced by humans who do not redraw the crooked lines of God.

CHAPTER NINE

The Ethnic Revival

Catholicism means here comes everybody.

James Joyce, *Finnegans Wake*

The most vigorous opponents of the so-called ethnic revival are the "official" intellectual and cultural leaders of the American church. Without knowing anything about the subject, and without having read anything but a chapter or two from Michael Novak (who has a data base of one respondent), such experts as Sidney Callahan, Abigail McCarthy, Donald Campion, Garry Wills, and Wilfrid Sheed assure us that the ethnic revival is a passing phenomenon and a bad one at that. It is a return to second-rate, the mediocre, the trivial. Who can learn anything from Poles and Italians anyhow?

In other words, just at the time when some people in the big world outside the church are beginning to discover certain fascinating aspects of American Catholic life, our own elites are denying the existence of ethnic diversity or hoping that it will all quickly go away.

To the extent that he is aware of this reaction, the communal Catholic is utterly baffled by it. In the ordinary world where he lives and works, ethnic diversity is and always has been taken for granted. What revival? he asks.

What revival indeed.

The quintessential paradox of this most paradoxical social development is that one can only begin to understand it when one realizes that it is not a revival at all but a rediscovery by cultural elites of something that has always existed. Wise and learned men, both sympathetic and antipathetic to the ethnic revival "movement" (which really isn't a movement either), have said many foolish and irrelevant things because they did not understand this paradox.

The present account must necessarily be somewhat autobiographical. I have been an ambivalent and rueful part of the ethnic revival. My interests have been mostly scholarly, to further greater understanding of the participants and the dynamics of the American pluralist experiment. I have not been concerned with generating Irish militancy, although I have been amused when some observers tried to exclude the Irish from the ranks of the ethnics.* Nor have I been searching for my Irish Catholic identity (of which I have been only too well aware all along); nor have I tried to persuade my fellow Irish Catholics that they are victims. To some extent we are, particularly among the cultural elites of American society; but the Irish don't feel victimized any more, and given the fact that they are the second most successful of the American religio-ethnic groups (Jews are first), maybe they have a point. Still, I could not have avoided being involved with other aspects of the ethnic revival. Ethnic was ethnic and that was that, especially as far as the funding agencies were concerned. No good social researcher turns away from a label that attracts funds. So while I disagree with some of the elements of the ethnic revival and am ambivalent about others, my account is still from the inside.

It all began with the discovery by America's journalistic, cultural, intellectual, and funding elites in the middle sixties that the easy and optimistic liberal assumption of rapid progress toward assimilation and integration in American society no longer seemed valid. Black militancy (a real but limited phenomenon) and black cultural pride (real and very extensive) and the white backlash (mostly a myth created to serve the emotional needs of the elites) all seemed to challenge the idea that the old irrational divisions of race, religion, and

---

*An exclusion which our empirical research shows to be absurd. For whatever it's worth, the Irish continue to be different from the American mainstream after four generations, and show no signs of giving up their bad habits.

nationality were vanishing in American culture. A substantial portion
of the elite conceded "separatism" and cultural pride to the "emerging" minorities but not to the "established" ones—to blacks,
browns, reds, and later, homosexuals and women—but not to Poles,
Italians, Irish, Germans, Greeks, etc., etc. Other members of the
elite made the astonishing discovery that all white Americans were
not members of the Jewish or British-American upper-middle class
and did not think like the writers of *The New York Time* editorials said
they should. Some of those discoverers were displeased and exasper-
ated, others were fascinated and began to think that the subject of
diversity in American society might be worth a closer look.

A few scholars, particularly historians, but also some sociologists
and political scientists (none of whom could get funds to study the
subject) were well aware of the persistence of diversity in the large
cities, small towns, and farm districts of the American republic.
These scholarly deviants found themselves in the interesting position
of being lectured by those who had rediscovered a subject to which
they had devoted a considerable amount of their professional ener-
gies. We held our tongues, however, because we saw the glitter of
gold in that rediscovery of diversity.

And that is fundamentally what the ethnic revival is: a rediscovery
of the fact of diversity by a cultural elite which had overlooked the
fact for several decades. It is essential to keep in mind that the so-
called ethnic revival had very little to do with anything that happened
in the ordinary daily lives of those who were called ethnics (no matter how one defines the term*). Indeed, if the truth be known, most
of the ethnics are not even aware of an ethnic revival and really
couldn't care less about it. They may dimly perceive that it is now
somewhat more socially approved to be proud of your heritage than it
was in the past. The ethnic, even the college educated ethnic (and our
research shows that a tremendous number of them are college educated), may be mildly pleased that the larger society has legitimated

---

*At the Center for the Study of American Pluralism we define ethnicity as diversity
not based on social class, age, or sex. To state it more positively, ethnicity is diversity
based on race, religion, national origin, language, or region.

a pride in one's heritage. Still, since most of them never stopped being proud of their heritages, the new legitimation is of little moment. Scholars, journalists, community organization leaders, officers of nationality associations, even an occasional artist and writer from the ethnic community, have found new freedom and new support in the ethnic revival. Some of them also have gained acceptance for a claim to be admitted to the ranks of the fashionably approved "victims." They might even have been amused to see such clearly ethnic characters as Baretta, Kojak, and Colombo appear on television. They might even rejoice mildly when children come home from school and talk about such things out of the ethnic past as Our Lady of Czechtohova or the Easter Rising. (What, after all, was the Easter Rising?) But beyond such minor changes and beyond the virtually inevitable interest by the third and fourth generations in their origins, the ethnic revival was and is an elite phenomenon.

The rediscovery of ethnicity is important because ethnicity is important in America. A greater understanding of the pluralism of our society is absolutely essential for social progress; but a good deal of what has been written about American ethnics could only have been produced by men who have confused reading, thinking, and talking *about* ethnics with actually living and talking *with* ethnics. In principle, of course, there is nothing wrong with intellectuals and quasi-intellectuals developing their own constructs that are not tested against reality. The trouble comes when they begin to confuse those constructs with reality.

A number of themes characterized the rediscovery of diversity:

1. *The ethnic as villain.* It was the Middle-American ethnics, the racists, the hard hats, the hawks who supported the Vietnam war and Richard Nixon. Of all the ethnics, the hard-hat ethnics (the construction workers) were the worst because they were the most hawkish and the most pro-Nixon. So the argument ran, and still does, in such journals as *Time* and *Newsweek,* the occasional passing comment on national TV, and in the infrequent article on the Op-Ed page of *The New York Times*. The image of the ethnic as hard-hat racist hawk is widely held among the nation's cultural and intellectual elites, and it

does not yield in the face of contrary data. The ethnic was rediscovered as the enemy of racial change, the enemy of reform in the Democratic party (which meant, of course, throwing the ethnics out), and the enemy of peace in Vietnam. He was alternately part of Middle America and part of the Establishment. The ethnic was the bad guy, the enemy of social progress, as one officer of a national association of social workers put it to me. The ethnic was a conservative, a reactionary, a relic of the past; he was also, though it was rarely stated explicitly, Catholic.

Now the evidence against this image is overwhelming. Catholics were more likely to be opposed to the war from the beginning than the mainstream of Americans. In a poll done in New York shortly after the famous Wall Street demonstration, construction workers were found to be the most likely to be opposed to the war. Ethnic scores on measures of racism are lower than the average for big cities in the North, and much lower, of course, than the national average. The ethnics did not over-defect from the Democratic party in 1972. On the contrary, their defection, if anything, was somewhat less than that of the average Democrat. Also, they turned against Nixon earlier and more strongly than did other segments of the American population after the Watergate revelations began. They continued to vote for liberal congressional candidates and be more on the liberal side of the national average on most social issues. One can, however, repeat these data until blue in the face, and they have no impact at all. The data are never effective in refuting religious convictions or myths which seem terribly important for the personality structures of those committed to them.

2. *The Wasp as scapegoat.* The mirror image of the ethnic as villain is the Wasp as scapegoat. It is repeated among many of the newer and younger "ethnic intellectuals." The Wasp is responsible for the plight of the ethnic. It is, after all, his society, his culture; and we have been grudgingly admitted into it as second-class citizens who must pay the price of admission by abandoning our own heritages. The Wasp—he's the enemy!

Doubtless there have been unfair assimilationist pressures on many of the immigrants, their children, and grandchildren in American society. Doubtless too there is a strong residue of anti-Catholic and antiethnic prejudice among the literary and cultural elites. Finally, commentators such as Wilfrid Sheed and Garry Wills, who seem to have turned against their heritage, are much more likely to be warmly received by the cultural elites than those who have remained loyal to their heritages.

But it is not valid or useful to scapegoat whole categories of people, particularly such an amorphous and undefined one as "Wasp," which can include everybody from Nelson Rockefeller to a dirt farmer in Oklahoma, from the Cabots and Lodges in Boston to the Nixon allies in Orange County, from a Georgia redneck to an Oregonian longshoreman. Indeed, at the Center for the Study of American Pluralism we have proscribed the word "Wasp," referring instead to "English Protestant" or "British Protestant." (And since Richard Rose has persuaded us that the only "British" are to be found in Ulster, we are more and more likely to use the former term rather than the latter.)

To scapegoat whole classes of people is sick. To search for an enemy who has victimized "us" (whoever "us" may be) is also sick. As a political style, scapegoating is little better than moral blackmail; as social analysis, it is little more than mythmaking; as social programming, it is blind, uninformed, and divisive. Besides, it was the English-Americans who let the rest of us in. They deserve our immense gratitude. They may have done it against their better judgment, they may have pressured us to become more like them, but they did let us in and never forced us to give up our heritages. To turn them into the enemy is a foolish and frivolous game, a residue of the romanticism of the 1960s that ought to be buried permanently in an unmarked grave.

3. *The organized ethnics.* From this perspective, ethnicity was to be used like race as an organizing principle for political and social action. The ethnics were to get their "house in order" or their "thing together"; having done so, they were to make common cause with

the blacks against the Establishment. The only trouble with this strategy was that there were already all kinds of Slavic-black alliances around the country, mostly presided over by the Democratic party (particularly, if I may be excused for mentioning it, in the Cook County Regular Democratic Organization, the biggest Polish-black alliance in all the world). Furthermore, there were already all kinds of ethnic organizations which had been doing business for years and which were not about to yield to newcomers who had discovered ethnicity for the first time. In most working-class and middle-class white neighborhoods, where community organization was attempted, more than one ethnic group existed. Finally, the appeal of ethnic militancy was not very attractive to most ethnics who simply did not like the political style of militancy when it was practiced by others. They were not about to get into it themselves. Under certain sets of circumstance and in some times and some places, the appeal to ethnic militancy did have some effect, although in the classic example of Newark the militant ethnic (Anthony Imperiale) has been repeatedly outfoxed, upstaged, and forced to moderation by the very sophisticated, traditional ward leader (Steve Addubato).

As the years have gone on, most of those who have been interested in organizing white urban groups to facilitate social change have steered away from exclusive reliance on ethnic appeal, though they may occasionally use it. Ethnicity, it turns out, is simply not in the same category as race in its power to motivate self-conscious activism.

4. *Better understanding of ethnics and their relationships.* This perspective is essentially scholarly. It seeks research methods, models, and data to understand the various components of American pluralistic society and polity and the interaction of these components with one another. This is the perspective of the Center for the Study of American Pluralism and its journal, *Ethnicity*. Those who work within this perspective have made, I think, considerable progress in the last five years. Political scientists, historians, and sociologists have produced a substantial body of research literature and have

begun to develop both theories and analytic models. Furthermore, an almost incredible number of younger scholars have begun to work in the area. When we began *Ethnicity* I was unconvinced that there would be enough articles for more than the first few issues. Now, we have more than 1,000 pages of manuscripts in our files. As far as I can see, there is no reason why this element of the ethnic revival should fade away.

The ethnic researcher still faces serious problems. A substantial part of the social science profession is not ready to concede the legitimacy of such research. (I am moved to ironic laughter by the uptight liberal scholar who insists on the moral obligation to do research on race but denounces research on other kinds of ethnic diversity as divisive.) Some scholarly journals reject articles on the subject out of hand (to the notable benefit of *Ethnicity*). Some academic departments will not hire or promote scholars who specialize in ethnic research, and many funding agencies would never consider supporting such projects. Things are not so bad now as they were ten years ago, but ethnicity is still not fully legitimate. The younger generation of scholars will change this state of affairs in due course, but I for one have grown more than a little weary of the fight. Each time an academic says to me that research in ethnicity is divisive, or that ethnic differences have gone away, or that no one is interested in such research, I find the temptation to poke him in the mouth growing ever stronger. One of these days I may succumb.

5. *Assert ethnic pride*. This component of the ethnic revival is to be found mostly among the leaders of the ethnic communities— organizational and cultural. Most of this emphasis comes from outside the national cultural elite, though occasionally an ethnic such as Michael Novak, who has made it into that elite, will argue ethnic pride. To be Polish, for example, is not only tolerable but good; jokes about Poles are an abomination. The Polish national trait is not stupidity and ignorance but wild, romantic passion. Copernicus was Polish, and Polish submarine crews in World War II were heroes, not clowns.

To feel resentment at stereotyping and to feel pride in one's heritage—even if one has to dig pretty deep into the past to find that heritage—have been characteristics of the immigrant groups since they first arrived on these shores. The ethnic revival has made it easier for the leaders of such groups to insist on proper recognition for ethnic heritages. (Despite the fact that the campaign against the propagation of Polish jokes has not been notably successful. One wonders what the reaction would have been had such jokes been told coast to coast against blacks or Latinos.)

Some of the manifestations of ethnic pride are interesting. Most of the immigrants who came from southern Italy at the end of the last century and the beginning of this one would have thought of themselves primarily in terms of their native provinces—Calabria, Naples, Sicily, Bari. They became Italian-Americans when the host society defined them as such and when they discovered the political and economic power to be obtained from such identification. More recently, however, many of them have begun to put the Italian tricolor on their car bumpers and to define themselves simply as Italian. But to their ancestors the tricolor was the flag of the hated Piedmontese oppression, an oppression that wiped out the old kingdom of Naples and produced a united Italy to which the southerners owed little allegiance. The Calabrians, in other words, only became Italians in the United States.

This feeling of cultural pride, now legitimated, will affect some ethnics more than others. It is likely to have its largest impact on younger scholars and artists coming from the ethnic communities. We may well have a flowering of literary and artistic productivity from these newly proud ethnic groups. Such a possibility can be excluded only if one maintains they have experienced nothing in the old country or in this one which is the proper subject of art, music, poetry, and fiction.

6. *The ethnic as victim.* This approach is merely the flip side of the coin of the Wasp as scapegoat. It is to be heard most frequently, I fear, from those scholars and intellectuals who in fact have not been

the victims of anything much at all, and who lead very comfortable
lives as tenured faculty members or as wandering interpreters of
American society. (Of course most of those who talk about blacks
and women being victims are not victims themselves either; they are
doing very nicely both economically and socially, thank you.) How
one responds to this theme of ethnic as victim depends upon how important the division of humankind into victims and victimizers is in
your world view. Most of those who propound the theory of ethnic
victimization are doing infinitely better than their cousins in the old
country and their ancestors in this—indeed, better than their cousins
in this country. It would be much more sensible and much more con-
structive to talk about the ethnic contribution instead of the ethnic as
victim. It is surely necessary to resist prejudice and bigotry (and
there is certainly much of that), but such resistance can occur without
appeals to the great suffering that one has experienced because of
prejudice.

7. *Quotas for ethnics*. The existence of "quotas," or the thinly
disguised substitute term, "affirmative action," is a tribute to the
capacity of lawyers, judges, bureaucrats, and Democratic party activists to violate the Constitution and to twist the laws of the land
without any statutory basis. Some leaders of the ethnic communities
are beginning to say that if there are to be quotas for blacks, browns,
reds, and women, then there ought to be quotas for them too. And if
there is to be affirmative action in finding senior faculty positions for
women and blacks at the great universities, so too there should be
affirmative action toward finding like positions for Irish, German,
Italian, and Polish Catholics.

The response of the scholarly community to this assertion has been
interesting. I have been told by colleagues that women and blacks are
underrepresented because of discrimination while Catholics are underrepresented because their religion prevents them from being good
scholars. Professor Galbraith and two of his cronies wrote an article
some time ago for *The New York Times Magazine* recommending
quotas for the blacks and women in American universities, arguing
indeed that the quota should be proportionate to the number of blacks

in a given community, not merely to the national average. I responded with an elaborate suggestion for a transformation of the Harvard faculty according to these criteria. Given the ethnic composition of the city of Cambridge, I argued, about ninety percent of the senior faculty positions at that worthy institution ought to be allotted to either the Italians or the Irish. Since there are so few Scot-Canadians in the Cambridge area, it would probably be necessary for Professor Galbraith to relinquish his chair. His response to my letter to the *Times* was to insist that census data showed that the Poles and the Italians were not being discriminated against in American society. The issue, of course, was not whether they were being discriminated against in the society at large but whether they were being discriminated against at the senior faculty level at Harvard University. The mind boggles at Professor Galbraith's ignorance of the fact that because the census cannot ask a religious question, about half of those labeled "Polish" are also Jewish.

There is surely anti-Catholicism at the upper level of America's intellectual elite, and the universities certainly ought to do something about their discrimination against Catholic scholars. But neither quotas nor affirmative action are effective ways of dealing with the problem. Indeed, given the overwhelming opposition to quotas in American society, the present rigid and dogmatic insistence on them by a small clique of liberal elitists will not survive—especially when those who allegedly benefit from quotas find that in the long run such policies are harmful rather than helpful. The black senior faculty member and the woman executive are just that from the point of view of most of their colleagues. They have been put in their positions to get the Feds off the institutions' backs without regard to whether they have the talent to fill their positions or not. With or without ability, they have to work extra hard against the assumption that they are there for reasons of policy only. Financially they may benefit as individuals, but from any other view they have been placed in an intolerable situation.

I have argued in this chapter that there is little ethnic militancy, indeed little consciousness among most ethnics about the so-called

ethnic revival. However, if the cultural elites of the country continue
to insist on affirmative action, then a time will come when this judgment will have to be changed, when it becomes clear to a substantial
number of ethnics—as it will eventually—that the goodies of the
society are being apportioned on the basis of such ascriptive factors
as race and sex, the ethnics are going to want to be dealt into the
game. They will fight vigorously if excluded.

    8. *The search for ethnic identity.* Partly out of envy of blacks,
who have a clear cultural identity, but mostly because it is a thing
that third and fourth generation people do, a considerable number of
younger American scholars and just plain undergraduate students
have become very interested in "rediscovering their ethnic identity."
This does not always mean, unfortunately, that they rediscover the
neighborhood in which they grew up; rather they rediscover something that existed further back in the past. One young Chicago journalist for whom I have a great deal of respect started out as a militant
new leftist. Within the space of a very few years he has turned into a
"communalist," that is to say, someone who is arguing that the
Cook County Democratic Organization *sans* corruption is the way
every big city ought to be run. In studying the operation of the
machine, he has discovered how much of his own cultural past was
involved with machine politics and has come to take a much more
benign (and in my judgment a much more accurate) view of the
communal approach to politics. Catholic scholars a decade older than
he have not been able to make such a rapid return to their roots. It
may well be that the ethnic revival has facilitated such a return for
ethnic intellectuals and just plain students, but it probably would
have happened anyway. I am inclined to think that this development
is irreversible. Interest in, sympathy toward, and pride about one's
heritage, as well as a search for future directions from past experience, have become options that are permanently available to those
young Americans who want them. This does not mean everybody or
even a majority of ethnics will become highly self-conscious of their
ethnicity (though the mean score in ethnic consciousness will probably move up), but it does mean that in our pluralistic society self-

conscious ethnicity is now a legitimate option for those who wish to exercise it.*

In addition to the various components of the ethnic revival a number of studies have marked the rediscovery of pluralism in American society. First of all, there are studies of specific groups, such as Richard Gambino's book about the Italians *(Blood of My Blood: The Dilemma of the Italian-American)* or my own book on the American Irish *(That Most Distressful Nation: The Taming of the American Irish)*. The Ford Foundation's interest in ethnicity stemmed from its concern about work and the working class in American society. This concern persists, although the foundation's interest in American pluralism is now much broader. Monsignor Geno Baroni of the National Center for Urban Ethnic Affairs has emphasized community organization in ethnic neighborhoods and, more recently, the development of new national umbrella organizations to bring more effective political pressures to bear on various public and private institutions. Irving Levine and the American Jewish Committee—in many ways the founders of the ethnic revival—have worked to a considerable extent out of the perspectives of intergroup relationships and of "consciousness raising" on the subject of diversity and pluralism. Michael Novak has pioneered the humanistic approach to ethnicity, particularly with his *Rise of the Unmeltable Ethnic*. Nathan Glazer and Daniel P. Moynihan, if they were not so young, could be called the grandfathers of the ethnic revival because of their phenomenally successful *Beyond the Melting Pot*. More recently they have begun to concentrate on the international manifestations of ethnicity in their new book to be published by the American Academy of Arts and Sciences.

Social scientists and historians, particularly those at the Center for

---

*Our research at the Center for the Study of American Pluralism shows that there is little correlation between ethnic self-consciousness and ethnically linked behavior. Those characteristics which differentiate among ethnic groups are not related to how self-consciously ethnic one might be. The Irish, for example, are excessive drinkers whether they are conscious of being Irish or not. They are also political activists regardless of their consciousness of Irish ethnicity.

the Study of American Pluralism, have worked on research projects to add to the meager body of knowledge that presently exists about American ethnic diversity. A number of younger writers, among them James Barry, William McCready, Ralph Whitehead, and Pastora Cafferty, have shown considerable interest in communalism as a basis for urban government and social policy.

It is fair to say, I think, that the approaches and the groups mentioned in the previous paragraphs represent the core of the positive approach to the rediscovery of pluralism. Although many others have joined the effort in recent years, if one wants a list of the groups and people who think that pluralism is a good thing in the United States and have worked to promote that conviction since the beginning of the revival, it appears above.

There have been four major responses to the ethnic revival: (1) simple nativism, (2) scholarly nativism, (3) responsible reservations, and (4) Catholic anti-Catholicism.

The *simple nativist* rejects on a priori grounds the possibility or the desirability of pluralism. Ethnicity, Naomi Bliven wrote in *The New Yorker,* is second-rate. The question, says William O'Neil in *The New Republic,* is whether there is too much ethnicity in American society; and would we be much better off if we were one ethnic group. Ethnic politics, *The New York Times* pontificates, is a virus brought to our country by the immigrants. Ireland, says C. V. Higgins in the *Boston Globe,* means merely mass, mud huts, and misery.

Ms. Bliven is a bit hard on Florence's Dante, Vienna's Mozart, and London's Shakespeare, to say nothing of Saul Bellow, James T. Farrell, and Eugene O'Neill. France is a one-ethnic group society; it seems not without internal problems. Interest-group politics was not invented by the ethnics but by James Madison; and C.V. Higgins is superb proof that a good mystery writer can also be a cultural ignoramus. The prejudices of the simple-minded nativists may be a problem for American pluralism, but such bigotry is impervious to the mitigating influence of dialogue.

The *scholarly nativist* is a slippery fellow. He suggests discreetly that the new interest in ethnicity is a reaction to the search for black power, and hence is part of a racist backlash. He hints that it may be intended to defend corrupt machine politics. He suggests that the assimilation process is far advanced in American society and enthusiastically endorses group consciousness among the new, approved minorities while doing his best to pretend that there is no reason or justification for group consciousness among the older ones. He ignores data, and if he works for a government agency he does his best to sabotage proposals for the collection of further data. Above all, he suggests, ethnicity is divisive and as such, it ought not to be mentioned in polite company.

Scholarly nativists are numerous in the social science professions. They are especially prevalent among those who are but a generation away from the immigrant neighborhood themselves. Having rejected their own heritages and unable to return home, they resent bitterly the suggestion that such a rejection may have been a mistake or even unnecessary. On the subject of the Catholic immigrant groups from Europe—they are bigots and in their heart of hearts many of them know it. With such people there can be no dialogue.

There are also several responsible observers who have expressed serious reservations about the ethnic revival. Among these *responsible reservationists* are Orlando Patterson, Harold Isaacs, Norman Podhoretz, and my friend and colleague, Arthur Mann. Patterson, Isaacs, and Mann have done extensive research on pluralism (indeed, all serve on the editorial board of *Ethnicity*). Podhoretz's stance within the Jewish community indicates that he is anything but an assimilationist. Still, the ethnic revival has made all of them uneasy. Patterson, a West Indian black sociologist on the faculty of Harvard, argues that ethnicity is "regressive," an attempt to turn back the evolutionary process, a rejection of the universalistic in favor of the particularistic, of the rational in favor of the nonrational. Good Enlightenment rationalist that he is, Patterson is appalled at such regression. Unlike many of his contemporary black scholars, he is ill at ease with black separatism, arguing that integration and assimilation are the enlightened, rational goal—the only one that really represents social progress.

142   THE COMMUNAL CATHOLIC

Isaacs, who has written brilliantly on the origin of ethnic identification, is extremely conscious of the fierce passions that ethnicity
can stir up. He fears that the renewed emphasis on pluralism may
unleash passions so powerful that the fabric of American society
could be in danger.

Arthur Mann, a distinguished historian whose students are doing
brilliant work analyzing the experience of immigrant groups in
American society, is disturbed by what he considers the irrational
romanticism of some of the ethnic revival enthusiasts. He sees the
revival to some extent as a product of the decline of rationality and
civility which afflicted the universities in the late 1960s.

Finally, Norman Podhoretz sees the emphasis on ethnic heritage
(whether from white ethnics or nonwhite ethnics) as a threat to
America's common culture.

The fears of all four are not without merit. A return to tribalism is
anything but attractive. One would not want to see the common culture denied or destroyed. One should properly be afraid of unleash-
ing primordial passions which would endanger the unity of American
society. Irrational and uncivil romanticism is diametrically opposed
to serious, scholarly research.

But all four are responding to some of the exaggerations of the
ethnic revival and to rhetoric which has no relationship to the reality
of American group life—rhetoric, be it noted, not invented by our
above-listed observers but by some undisciplined ethnic enthusiasts.

To Professor Patterson I would respond* that the universal and
particular are not contradictory but complementary. Most human behavior represents a dialectic or a dialogue between the local and the
cosmopolitan, the traditional and the modern, the particular and the
universal. One comes to know the ground one stands on not to remain there but to make it a base from which to move out into the
world.

*In fact I have responded at a debate meeting of the American Academy of Arts and
Sciences in Boston, 1974, chaired by Daniel P. Moynihan. Much to my surprise, I had
the impression that that very elitist audience was more on my side than on
Patterson's—enough so to make me wonder whether I was on the right side after all.

To Professor Isaacs I would say that the marvel of American society is that unlike most multiethnic societies in the world it has been able to cope relatively well with diversity. The ethnic revival is not an attempt to sharpen differences among groups but to understand better the differences that exist and the protocols, institutions, processes, and dynamisms by which these differences have been harmonized. The ethnic separatists have no audience in their communities, and it is unthinkable that the ethnic masses would want to withdraw from American society. On the contrary, it is *their* society; if anything, they may be too uncritically proud of it.

To Mr. Podhoretz I would say that sure, there's a common culture, but ethnicity is not a way of distinguishing oneself from that culture. It is rather a way of dealing oneself into it. In a complex, pluralistic society, you've got to be *something,* and ethnic groups came into being not as a backward look to the Old World but as a dynamic means of finding a place in the New World. From the very beginning, the immigrants saw no conflict between being an American and being Irish, German, Italian, Jewish, Lithuanian, Czech, Armenian, or Luxembourger. Room for pluralism is in fact part of the common culture.

And to my friend Professor Mann—from whom I have learned so much about ethnic diversity—I would say that I can understand how the uncivil and romantic enthusiasts upset him. They are opposed to everything he believes about the civility and rationality of the university. If I am less upset than he, the reason is that in my experience, perhaps, the university is substantially less civil and rational than he has found it to be. Even some of the internationally known experts on civility turn out to be very uncivil indeed. I don't like romantic enthusiasts either; but I don't think that they have much following in the rank-and-file ethnic communities, and I don't take them very seriously. They are not a threat to the healthy functioning of American pluralism; and if they are a trial to the university, it may well be a trial brought about by the university itself. I can understand Professor Mann's chagrin at the enthusiasts who announce that they have "discovered" ethnic diversity. Professor Mann and his colleagues at the

Oscar Handlin School of Immigrant History have been studying it for many decades.

Implicit in much of the discussion above is the dilemma of assimilation versus cultural pluralism. Is America to be a homogenous society or a mosaic society? Is America to be a country in which everyone becomes like everyone else or a country in which sharp dividing lines are drawn among ethnic groups? The nativist, simple or scholarly, is an out and out assimilationist. The ethnic enthusiasts are committed cultural pluralists. The serious critics acknowledge, but are uneasy about, the fact of pluralism and appalled by the naive enthusiasm of those who do not understand its dangers.

Those of us who have come down on the side of cultural pluralism and are less uneasy than the four responsible critics I discussed above feel now that the alternative of either cultural pluralism or assimilation appears to be a false one in the United States. The critical difference between ethnic pluralism in America and that in most other countries of the world is that the boundaries among the various groups in the American society are remarkably permeable, and ethnicity is an option rather than an obligation.

The *Catholic* anti-Catholics can be described briefly. Both the intellectual and social action elites of the American Catholic church were profoundly suspicious of the ethnic revival. Many of the social action elites viewed it as an attempt to rationalize white ethnic racism. The intellectual elites, only recently admitted into the mainstream of American culture (and then as second-class citizens), were highly incensed that anyone could see anything good in the Catholic culture they had just left behind. Part of the viciousness of the attack on Michael Novak by Garry Wills, Wilfrid Sheed, Daniel and Sydney Callahan, and Peter Steinfeld surely results from the fact that they (and others in the *Commonweal* magazine group) view Novak as an apostate from the newly found liberal faith.

Some of the social action elites have clearly been won over in part because Monsignor Geno Baroni was one of their own number and in part because such old social-action leaders as Monsignor John Egan and Father Philip Murnion have grasped, with their characteristically

acute perceptions, that elements of the ethnic revival resonate very
well with the powerful instincts of Catholic social activism.

But still the American church has largely ignored the ethnic revival. The hierarchy pretends that it does not exist and mentions not a
word about ethnicity in its description of the present state of the
American church which it submitted to the 1974 Synod of Bishops in
Rome. Catholic journals—*America, Commonweal, U.S. Catholic,
St. Anthony's Messenger,* the *Critic,* the *National Catholic Reporter*
—pay scant attention to the ethnic revival. They do not seem to understand even yet its fundamental assumption that there is much in
the American Catholic experience of value and relevance to contemporary problems. The fashion of attacking American Catholicism or
ridiculing it (as in Tom McHale's black-humor novels, *Principato*
and *Farrigan's Retreat,* and the cartoons in the *Critic,* and that intol-
erably bad novel, *The Last Catholic in America*) has such a strong
grip on the cultural elite of the American church that one fears it will
be a long time before the fashion is changed.

But, obviously, the ethnic revival has involved Catholics. Many of
the ethnics who were the subject of the revival were the members of
Catholic immigrant groups. Not a few of those involved in the multiple manifestations of that revival were Catholic. Even if the official
church and the Catholic elites ignore the phenomenon, still it is having an ever increasing impact on American Catholicism. But more
than this must be said, I think. Out in the grass roots of the American
church they may not have called it ethnicity, they may never have
used the words cultural pluralism, but they knew all about the
phenomenon. American Catholicism, for at least this century, has
been a pluralistic microcosm in which many of the strains and
dynamisms, the forces and the counterforces of America's pluralist
society have been at work with exaggerated intensity. American
Catholicism was and still is a superb laboratory for the study of
pluralism at work. Scholars, social policymakers, and practitioners
could have a glorious time investigating puralism in the American
Catholic experience if they so desired.

I have often been asked when I "rediscovered" ethnicity. My

answer is that if you grew up on the west side of Chicago in the
1930s, went through the Chicago seminary in the 1940s and '50s,
and served in parishes of the Chicago archdiocese in the '50s
and '60s, you never had to rediscover ethnicity; it was there all
along. From the point of view of the Chicago neighborhood ethnic,
the amazing thing is that anyone had to rediscover it. How could they
ever have missed it in the first place?

In my neighborhood there were Catholics and Protestants, Irish,
Germans, Italians, and Swedes. In the seminary I went to there were
Irish, Germans, Poles, Italians, Lithuanians, Slovaks, Slovenes,
Czechs, Ukranians, Croatians, Dalmatians, Luxembourgers, and
blacks. Most of these came from national parishes and had an approach to Catholicism and a style of Catholic practice that was at
odds with my own. It was not so much that I had to learn to tolerate
this diversity; it was as natural as the air we breathe or the red street-
car we rode to school. We took it for granted that our classmates
would return to the kinds of parishes from which they came and practice a kind of Catholicism there which was both like and unlike our
own (under the benign administration of an Irish archbishop, of
course, or possibly a German one). I was told in whispered tones
when I asked about this diversity (troublemaker even then) that it was
something we had to tolerate or there would be schism. Obviously,
policy decisions had been made in the past. The tolerance may have
been reluctant, and the treatment of the non-Irish components of the
Chicago archdiocese may have been less than equitable; still whatever its faults and frailties, the pluralism of the archiocese of Chicago
was remarkably adroit. It was able to stitch together "Americanization" and "minority rights" within a structure which if not exactly
flawless, at least did not come apart at the seams. In retrospect, it
was, and is, an extraordinary achievement.

Without realizing it, we had found an alternative perspective, a
third way which lay somewhere between assimilation and cultural
pluralism, a version of John Higham's "pluralistic integration."
While there was some confidence that with time the Poles, for example, would be less suspicious of the rest of us, there was relatively

little attempt to hurry the process. In the early days of the seminary, many of my classmates from Polish parishes had learned their religion in Polish and received report cards in Polish to take home to their parents. (Such report cards were used in the archdiocese of Chicago until 1950.)

Much of the history of American Catholicism is concentrated on the exciting years between 1880 and 1900, and in particular on the famous Cahensley memorial, an attempt on the part of a group of Catholics in Germany to obtain separatist privileges for German Catholics in America. The "official" doctrine in Catholic history was that "Cahensleism" was dangerously close to heresy, and that the "Americanizers"—Cardinal Gibbon, Archbishop Ireland, Archbishop Keene—were the heroes of the fray. More recently, the work of Colman Barry has described the plight of the German-Americans much more sympathetically and recognized the legitimacy of their claims. Unfortunately, however, both perspectives are blind to the de facto situation which existed in most dioceses then and at most times since the Cahensley controversy. Careful research today (especially by Charles Shanabruch under the direction of Arthur Mann) shows that the responses of the archdiocese of Chicago on a day to day, week to week, year to year basis to the challenges presented by the national parishes were remarkably adroit. There were dissatisfied parishes, of course. There was a notable defection of Ukranian Catholic parishes when the Irish hierarchy banned a married clergy; there was the schism which produced the small Polish National Church. But whatever the mistakes, whatever the injustices, the enterprise held together.

Bishops Feehan and Quigley, whose decisions Shanabruch critically but sympathetically analyzes, were not theorists. They were simple men with very serious problems of diversity. They had to respect the integrity of the multiple ethnic groups within their diocese. They also had to preserve the unity of the archdiocese and to facilitate the adjustment of the immigrants to American life. Finally, they had to respond to the virulent nativism that characterized much of American life during the time of the notorious Dillingham Commission and the repressive immigration laws. With some mistakes and some injustices—usually unintentional—they managed to pull it off. Quigley believed, in principle, that the immigrants were entitled to keep many of their customs, but neither man was interested in drawing sharp lines. A vague and messy archdiocese was much better than one torn apart by schism. I suspect that as more and more monographs are written about the Catholic church and immigration, this style of tolerating—and perhaps even enjoying—the ambiguity of such a fantastically pluralistic church will be seen to have been commonplace.

It is fashionable now to criticize the Irish hierarchy. Italians like Gambino and Rudolph Vecoli of the University of Minnesota, Slavs like Michael Novak, and renegade Irishmen like Robert Sam Anson describe the Irish hierarchy as oppressive, stupid, and insensitive. Some of the new national ethnic clergy organizations are reluctant to admit Irish members, and spend a good deal of their time bitching about Irish control.

Yet I must ask whether there was any other ethnic group which had the pragmatism, the political skill, and the ability to work amidst the ambiguity and uncertainty that the Irish did. Could the Germans, for example, or the French (who once did dominate the American church), or even the native American bishops (who ruled Baltimore in the early part of the nineteenth century) could they have carried out the pluralistic game so adroitly? I agree with Philip Gleason: "If not the Irish, then who?"

But the Irish need no defense, and when Italians like Gambino and Vecoli criticize the Irish hierarchy, I very quickly point out to them that if Irish bishops, archbishops, and cardinals are frequently insensitive and inept, the proper place to launch the complaint is with the Italian apostolic delegate and the Italian popes who are responsible for their appointment.*

*It is worth noting, incidentally, that the present president of the National Conference of Catholic Archbishops is Italian; his predecessor was Polish and the first president was Welsh.

The pluralism of the American Catholic church and the pluralism of its predominantly Irish hierarchy was instinctive, pragmatic, unselfconscious, unreflective. It made lots of mistakes; it was insensitive on occasion to minority groups; it frequently was horrendously anti-intellectual. Yet, for all these weaknesses, Catholic pluralism in the United States was a success. There were few schisms, the ethnic immigrants remained Catholic and remained ethnic while becoming American. This phenomenon is so much part of the environment in which all of us have grown up that we must take a long step backward to see it in its proper perspective. When we finally do obtain perspective, I would submit, the achievement is breathtaking. Catholic pluralism in the United States shouldn't have worked. Intellectuals inside and outside of the church deny that it has worked; and yet the Irish, the Italians, the Poles, the Germans, the Lithuanians, Czechs, Slovaks, Slovenes, Croatians, French (both Canadian and Cajun), the Armenians, Ukranians, Lebanese are for the most part still Catholic, still ethnic, and yet very much American. The church, of course, didn't do it alone; it was helped by the political organizations and by the culture of the host society which, at least in one of its manifestations, tolerated and even encouraged pluralism. Still, it worked when it shouldn't have.

On balance the rediscovery of pluralism has been a benign event for American society. Four cardinal principles of American life are clearer now than they have been for a long time:

1. The American creed argues that anyone can be an American no matter what his race, his religion, his nationality, his cultural background so long as he commits himself to the fundamental political principles of American society. Indeed, until the early part of the twentieth century it was not even necessary to speak English to become an American. The creed is not always honored in practice, but it is closer to being honored now than ever before.

2. For the overwhelming number of American citizens group identification is not a way of separating themselves from the common culture, the common polity, the common social structure, but rather a way of defining themselves into it. Ethnicity is only concerned in a

150 THE COMMUNAL CATHOLIC

minor way with remembrances of things past. It is a way of claiming for yourself part of the American social turf, a turf shared with all other Americans.

3. American politics and social action are achieved not by preaching apocalypse, not by exhorting to guilt, not even primarily by legal decision through which a minority imposes its will on everyone else. Progress and social change are accomplished in American society by building coalitions whose importance cannot be ignored. The art of coalition building—often termed and frequently sneered at as "ethnic politics"—is absolutely essential in American group life. Compromise, consensus, respect for the vital interests of all components of the coalition—these are the essence of American political and social life. None of the ethnics are interested in destroying this way of doing things. The only real enemies of coalition-building politics are some of the American intelligentsia, and not infrequently those very intellectuals who have such contempt for ethnics.

4. The health and welfare of the coalition is never served by demanding that any major component group in it sacrifice its absolutely vital self-interest. When such a demand is made by leadership of the whole society, by other groups, or by certain morally concerned and religiously righteous members within the group, then more harm than good will inevitably result.

The ethnic revival has made these four principles so clear that it would be difficult indeed to deny them. In addition, it has relieved some of the pent up tension of the new generation of intellectuals coming out of the ethnic communities who find themselves caught between pride in and loyalty toward their origins, and the perennial demand of the American cultural elite that the ethnic intellectual turn against his past. In years gone by this demand was not resisted; more recently, young intellectuals have begun to resist it. The ethnic revival provides them with a rationale for doing so.

CHAPTER TEN

A Theology of Pluralism

The communal Catholic knows instinctively that pluralism and diversity are part of the warp and woof of human life. He also knows that Catholicism is in its best moments sympathetic to pluralism. To the extent that he can remember his papal social encyclicals from college days, he recollects that the popes were for pluralism too. Hence, the emphasis on pluralism, diversity, neighborhoods, and family life which he hears from the ethnic revivalists resonate well with his own hunches and inclinations. But he also knows that those who see diversity leading to conflict have a point too. How does one reconcile unity and diversity? And come to think of it, that sounds like a question from college days as well. What was the answer we learned then? And how do we approach it now?

Charles Meyer, in his important study of the priesthood, *Man of God,* has suggested that we are moving from a mystadelic to a mystagogic age—from a time of explaining mysteries as indigestible chunks of the irrational in the midst of an otherwise totally explicable universe to a time when we try to probe the richness of the mystery as a revelation of a great secret about the universe. There are, I take it, three great mysteries: the mystery of being—why is there anything at all? The mystery of good and evil—why the titanic war in heaven between good and evil where good is always on the brink of defeat?

And the mystery of the one and the many—why does unity exist amidst so much diversity? The question of pluralism, it seems to me, must be subsumed under the mystery of the one and the many.

There are three aspects of this mystery. (1) The philosophical question of whether the *one* exists in the *many* or of whether the *many* exist in the *one*. (2) The sociopolitical question of how one harmonizes diversity and unity in a society. Does one create unity by homogenization or by the integration of diversity? Does one try to repress diversity or does one (to use the current word fashionable among the still powerful assimilationist forces in our society) "celebrate" diversity? (3) The theological question of why God chose to have the *many* as diverse as they are. And it is this question which is the principal concern of this chapter. Why is there so much diversity? Why did God choose to have the *many* as diverse as they are?

God created with seemingly mad exuberance. From our human viewpoint there is too much creation altogether—too many stars, too many galaxies, too many billions of light years, too many species of plants, animals, fish, birds, insects, germs, viruses; too many races among humankind, too many languages, too many cultures, too many religions. It would have been much more sensible to have limited the number of all those things to a manageable size. Wouldn't one race, one language, one religion have been enough? At the risk of being somewhat anthropomorphic (but then everyone must who tries to speak of God), one might characterize God as "showing off," creating with reckless abandon, spewing forth diversity in life in senseless superabundance, so as to impress us with his powers and his ingenuity. As a poet has suggested to me, "Perhaps God was drunk." "What," I asked the poet, "could ever inebriate the Deity?" "Why, love," she replied. "What else?"

But it is also clear that sin is deeply involved in the phenomenon of diversity. Let us leave aside the physical disasters caused by conflicts among the diverse physical forces of the planet—water, air, drifting plates in the earth's crust, volcanic action. (Although if one follows the process theologians, one must concede that even these forces are operating with a God-given freedom of their own.) We merely have to read the daily newspapers to see how much of the suffering and horror of the human condition is caused by primordial differences of race, religion, language, nationality, custom, sex, and age. The front page wars of the last three decades—principally in Vietnam and Korea—may have been fought over ideology. They may have been struggles between capitalism and socialism, though surely primordial elements were also at work. But the back-page wars have been far more bloody, causing perhaps twenty million deaths. The primordial conflicts in Indonesia, Sri Lanka, Malaysia, India at the time of partition, Bangladesh, the Congo, Ruanda, Urundi, the Sudan, Iraq, Cyprus, Palestine, Biafra, and Ulster are not conflicts over how the economy should be organized, but conflicts about the raw, primal diversities which have led men to murder each other from the very beginning.

We began, presumably, with a nice village on the bank of a river. The only trouble was that down the river, around the bend, was another village made up of people who were savages and barbarians. How did we know that? Why because they painted their faces blue, and all civilized people like us painted their faces yellow. We thought about it for a while and realized that it was very likely those strangers were planning to attack us. Therefore we decided to attack them first. Sure enough, halfway down the path on the river bank we encountered their war party coming to kill us.

And so it has been down through human history. Few men will die willingly for ideology, but tens of thousands will die over the differences of skin color and the date of celebration of Easter, for infant baptism or use of pig fat on rifle bullets. How simple it all would be to have done with differences, to live as one race with one religion and one culture and one language. Indeed, the great Scholastic theologians of the Middle Ages concluded—largely from the tower of Babel myth—that if it were not for sin there would be no diversity in the human condition. The fantastic pluralism we find in the cultures of the world, in other words, is at best a necessary evil intended not by God but caused by human sinfulness.

It was easy enough for the Scholastics to subscribe to such a posi-

tion because they had only very limited notions of the sheer amount
of diversity to be found within the human condition. More recently,
continental Catholic theologians have begun to develop a theology of
pluralism that attempts to legitimate both pluralistic theological approaches and also the compatability of Christianity with various
world cultures. At Louvain University in 1972 there was an international colloquy on "Pluralism and Communication." Many of the
papers presented there have been published in the journal, *Pro Mundi
Vita,* entitled "Pluralism, Polarization and Communication in the
Church" (45:1973). What is striking about this symposium, and particularly about its most important paper by Jan Kerkhofs, is that
while the participants were quite willing to see the global issue of
pluralism (Christianity in India, Christianity in South Africa, etc.),
they seemed quite unaware of the pluralism going on right outside
the windows of their conference. Not a word was said about the
Walloon-Flemish pluralism of Belgium, which threatened to tear the
country apart and which indeed had just succeeded in tearing the
University of Louvain apart. Nor was there a word about the
pluralism in their midst created by the Gastarbeiters, the immigrant
workers, whom the social democracies of Western Europe ruthlessly
exploit in order that they might keep their economic prosperity going. Pluralism, in other words, was off in the far corners of the
world, not just down the street.

Yet, of course, the ones we have the most problems with are those
who are most like us. It would be very hard for a North American to
distinguish between a Yoruba, a Hausa, or an Ibo in Nigeria. Similarly, a Nigerian would have to spend a considerable amount of time
in Canada before he could distinguish between a French- or an
English-Canadian, to say nothing of an Italian-Canadian. And while
no one in Ulster has any difficulty telling who is Catholic and who is
Protestant, both the Canadian and the Nigerian would be utterly
baffled to distinguish them in that hate-filled province. It is not just
the stranger on the other side of the world who threatens us, it is also
the stranger down the street, around the corner, across the river.

But also, much of the richness and the creativity of the human condition comes from the particularities of distinctive cultures. American Indian jewelry, Thai silk, Indian saris, Irish whiskey, Italian food, Jewish humor, Polish passion, American black music—the world would be bland and dull indeed were it to be deprived of this rich diversity. Shakespeare was not a Western European, not an Anglo-Saxon, not a Briton, perhaps not even an Englishman; he was, during his creative years, a Londoner. And Dante was not a citizen of the Mediterranean civilization, of the Latin culture, of Italy, or even of Tuscany; he was a Florentine. Mozart was not a Teuton, or a German, or an Austrian; he was first a Salzburger and then a Viennese. And Jesus himself was not a Roman, or a Hellene, or a Palestinian but a Galilean. The greatness of all the contributions of all these men was shaped to a substantial extent by the particularities of the tiny spectrum of the time-space continuum on which they stood. They indeed transcended such limitations and spoke to all men of all ages, but their transcendence did not come from denying their own cultural roots but rather from seeing the richness and the universality that was latent in their own cultural heritage. The great creators, in other words, were not alienated men cut off from their own past and their own community. To descend to a much lower level of achievement, Harold Abramson pointed out in an article in the *Columbia University Forum* that the trouble with the Nixon White House may well be that it had no ethnic roots.

We therefore have the paradox of human diversity: much of what is evil and much of what is good in the human condition comes from the fact that we are different biologically, socially, culturally, linguistically, religiously, psychologically. Why does God tolerate such a paradox?

I would argue that the richness of human diversity is merely a reflection of the richness and superabundance of all creation, a manifestation of the overwhelming, overflowing goodness and power of the divine love. It is human sinfulness which refuses to rejoice over and revel in this diversity, leading us instead to be frightened of those who are different and to strike out to destroy them before they can destroy us.

Or to put the matter in a parable, God and the angels had a great party one night, and at the end of it God announced he was going to create humankind. The angels warned him that there would be nothing but trouble from such a creation, but he insisted; and because the party had been a splendid success, he decided he would impress the angels with his abilities by creating them in a welter of diversity. "Look!" he cried, "at those flashing brown eyes, that crooked nose, that red hair. At that tall, thin creature, at that short, stocky one! How about that fantastically gutteral language or that beautifully melodic one? Look at all those weird crazy customs! Look at all those costumes! Look at all those kinds of hair—straight, curly, kinky, light, dark! Aren't the skins beautiful—light, dark, black, pink, brown, and everything in between? Isn't it marvelous? What a joke!" And the Angels, dutiful creatures that they were, laughed long and loud, even though personally they were a bit uneasy. And so God and the angels went off to do other things. The next morning God looked down on his splendidly diverse creation and discovered that human beings were fighting over the differences he had created for their enjoyment. "My God," (you should excuse the expression) he said, "they didn't get the joke!"

To which humankind might have replied with the words of Robert Frost: "Lord, forgive the little jokes/ I've played on thee, And I'll forgive the great big one/you played on me."

The father of humankind must have reasoned much as Phyllis McGinley suggests he did:

Adam, perhaps, while toiling late,
     With life a book still strange to read in,
Saw his new world, how variegate,
     And mourned, "It was not so in Eden,"
Confusing thus from the beginning
Unlikeness with original sinning.*

It was to restore the unity destroyed by human sin that Jesus came into the world. To pursue the fanciful rhetoric of my parable, it was to persuade humankind to see the humor of God's joke that Jesus arrived on the scene. That he intended for there to be unity among his followers is so obvious from reading the Scriptures that one need not elaborate on the point. The Last Supper prayer of Jesus over his disciples removes the matter from debate.

However, the unity that Jesus sought was not to be achieved by homogenization or the elimination of diversity. In the ecstatic religious experience that is recorded for us in the Pentecost story, the enthusiasm of the followers of Jesus is not such that everyone speaks one language but rather that all the diverse peoples hear the message of God's love each in his *own language*. The Parthians and Medes and the Elamites and the inhabitants of the parts of Libya about Cyrene, and all those other strange characters that pass briefly before our eyes in the second chapter of Acts continue to be Parthians and Medes, Elamites and inhabitants of the parts of Libya about Cyrene, to say nothing of Phrygians, Pamphylians, Cretans, and Arabians.

Similarly, St. Paul's vision of Christian unity in Galatians is neither male nor female, Jew nor Gentile, Cretan nor Roman but all one in Christ Jesus. That can scarcely be taken to imply that the biological differences between males and females will be eliminated. Hence it seems to admit the persistence of differences between Jews and Gentiles and Greeks and Romans. The whole context of his ministry, however, indicates that he had no illusions about the persistence of diversity in the human condition. Indeed, any call to "restore all things in Christ" can scarcely be a call for the elimination of the richness and the diversity that mark the human condition. We will achieve unity in the midst of diversity by seeing the point of the divine joke and not by abolishing the joke.

Unity in Christ, then, is a good to be achieved in loving service which respects the authenticity of diversity. It is not a goal to be achieved through artificially and externally imposed uniformity. The stranger who is different from us is the Lord Jesus. Hence we must serve him, listen to him, learn from him. Kerkhofs sums it up nicely:

1. Instead of striving after uniformity the Church should constantly try to evoke and stimulate man's creativity, to encourage and maintain diversity in communion and communion in diversity. As in the relationship between married partners, or between generations or cultures, both these factors are equally vital, and to overrate one at the expense of the other can only lead to imbalance, injustice and heresy.

2. It follows that, as the Church is today growing out of the cocoon of a static culture, described by the word "christendom" in history, it will have to guide Christians towards an acceptance of this diversity as a basic and constitutive value of man, as an individual and in groups, but at the same time it has to encourage new ways of fostering communion, of understanding the Stranger, and all those strangers whom He represents.*

Faced with the ambiguity of human diversity, which provides both richness and suffering for humankind, is there a symbol in the Christian symbol system which resonates with this pluralism and illuminates its ambiguity so as to indicate directions for our lives? In response to this Tillichean question, I would suggest that the Christian system which correlates best with the phenomenon of human pluralism is that of the Holy Spirit.

For the Holy Spirit is the dimension of the godhead that represents richness, variety, abundance. When the Spirit speaks to our spirit he speaks to that which is most creative, most original in each of us, and therefore he stirs up a superabundance of creative diversification. If the Spirit is to call out the best in each of us, and if each of us is unique and special, then the work of the Spirit is not a work of bland homogenization but rather one of wild, glorious differentiation.

The Holy Spirit could be thought of as a kind of divine Tinkerbell, flitting through space, whirling, twirling, spinning, leaping, diving, prancing, dancing, hand clapping, darting, sparking forth from his divine wand flashes of divine creativity from whatever it touches.

*"Pluralism, Polarization and Communication in the Church—Some Theological Aspects," Jan Kerkhofs, S.J., *Pro Mundi Vita* 45, 1973, p. 5.

The Holy Spirit is a laughing spirit, a poltergeist, a spirit who in mother Ireland is a leprechaun.

For the United States of America such a theological vision of pluralism, however inadequate and amateurish it may be, ought to be of capital importance. Madison and his colleagues decided to make virtue out of necessity. As Gordon Wood has pointed out in his *Creation of the American Republic 1776–1887,* it was believed in the early 1770s that when tyranny was removed a republic of virtue would emerge in which everyone willingly and graciously would yield his own particular good for the common good of all. But by the time the Americans assembled in Philadelphia to write the Constitution, they were older, sadder, and wiser men. They had seen the state constitutions, they had seen the Articles of Confederation, and they realized that the diverse group interests were not eliminated from the society. The tyranny of a majority group over a minority group was every bit as bad as that of a minority over the majority. So they deliberately designed a society which could only govern itself by coalition building. And Madison, in his tenth and fifty-first Federalist Papers, laid out such a theory of a coalition-building society. America was already a pluralistic nation; Madison and his colleagues turned that fact to their advantage. In *People of Paradox,* Michael Kammen suggests:

And so it was that American colonial history, which had begun with a quest for purity and homogeneity, ended with a sophisticated rationale for pluralism and heterogeneity. What had happened was not really so paradoxical as it may seem, for the so-called melting pot had been a boiling cauldron all along, from Jamestown to James Madison. There is a very real sense in which the American nation emerged, not in response to new-found national unity, but rather in response to provincial disunity, in response to a historical problem of long duration: how best to control unstable pluralism, how best to balance the areas of compulsion and freedom in American life.*

---

*Michael Kammen, *People of Paradox* (New York: Alfred A. Knopf, Inc., 1972), pp. 73–74.

It was the Madisonian vision of government through a coalition of groups that made it possible for the later immigrants to come to these shores, coalesce into ethnic groups (which are dynamic new creations of the American environment and not throwbacks to an Old World culture), and through these ethnic groups win a place for themselves in the polity, the economy, and the society of their new nation. The hyphen in the hyphenated American is in fact an equality sign. The greatest of the American political philosophers understood this phenomenon of the hyphen as equal sign a long time ago. As he commented to his friend Hinnissy:

An Anglo-Saxon, Hinnissy, is a German that's forgot who was his parents. . . . I'm an anglo-Saxon. . . . Th' name iv Dooley has been th' proudest Anglo-Saxon name in th' County Roscommon f'r many years. . . . Pether Bowbeen down be th' Frinch church is formin' th' Circle Francaize Anglo-Saxon club, an' me ol' frind Dominigo . . . will march at th' head iv th' Dago Anglo-Saxons whin th' time comes. There ar're twinty thousan' Rooshian Jews at a quarther a vote in th' Sivinth Ward; an', ar-rmed with rag hoods, they'd be a tur-r-ble thing f'r anny inimy iv th' Anglo-Saxon 'lieance to face. Th' Bohemians an' Pole Anglo-Saxons may be a little slow in wakin' up to what th' pa-apers calls our common hurtage, but ye may be sure they'll be all r-right whin they're called on. . . . I tell ye, whin th' Clan an' th' Sons iv Sweden an' th' Banana Club an' th' Circle Francaize an' th' Pollacky Benivolent Society an' th' Coffee Clutch that Schwartzmeister r-runs an' th' Tur-rnd' yemind an' th' other Anglo-Saxons begin f'r to raise their Anglo-Saxon battle cry, it'll be all day with th' eight or nin people in th' wurruld that has th' misfortune iv not bein' brought up Anglo-Saxons.*

Claude Levi-Strauss remarked somewhere that in primitive tribes with totemic clans the animals are always of the same order. Lions, tigers, panthers are in one tribe while hawks, falcons, and eagles

*Finley P. Dunne, *Mr. Dooley in Peace and in War* (Boston: Scholarly Press, 1898), pp. 54–56.

may be in another, but never lions and falcons, hawks and tigers, panthers and eagles in the same tribe. Levi-Strauss takes this to be evidence that human society is structured not by homogenization but by diversification as a prelude to later integration. One need not buy the whole structuralist approach to see the wisdom and even the beauty in Levi-Strauss's insight. It is the contention of this chapter that such an insight is far from foreign to Christian theology (to say nothing of Catholic theology, which ought by definition to argue that the church is "for everybody"). The insights of Levi-Strauss, Madison, and Martin Dooley are perfectly compatible with it. So, too, are the Spirit-inspired verses of Phyllis McGinley:

Rejoice that under cloud and star
    The planet's more than Maine or Texas.
Bless the delightful fact there are
    Twelve months, nine muses, and two sexes;
And infinite in earth's dominions
Arts, climates, wonders, and opinions.

Praise ice and ember, sand and rock,
    Tiger and dove and ends and sources;
Space travelers, and who only walk
    Like mailmen round familiar courses;
Praise vintage grapes and tavern Grappas,
And bankers and Phi Beta Kappas;

● ● ●

Praise the disheveled, praise the sleek;
    Austerity and hearts-and-flowers;
People who turn the other cheek
    And extroverts who take cold showers;
Saints we can name a holy day for
And infidels the saints can pray for.

Praise youth for pulling things apart,
    Toppling the idols, breaking leases;
Then from the upset apple-cart
    Praise oldsters picking up the pieces.
Praise wisdom, hard to be a friend to,
And folly one can condescend to.
Praise what conforms and what is odd,
    Remembering, if the weather worsens
Along the way, that even God
    Is said to be three separate Persons.
Then upright or upon the knee,
Praise Him that by His courtesy,
For all our prejudice and pains,
Diverse His Creature still remains.*

*From *The Love Letters of Phyllis McGinley*. Copyright © 1953 by Phyllis McGinley. Reprinted by permission of The Viking Press, Inc. and Martin Secker & Warburg Ltd.

CHAPTER ELEVEN

The Survival of the
Catholic Schools

Perhaps the most astonishing finding of the 1974 NORC survey of attitudes towards Catholic schools is that ninety percent of the American Catholics favor the continuation of such schools and eighty percent would increase their annual contribution to keep the schools going—fifty percent by more than $50 a year and twenty-five percent by more than $100 a year. Nor is there any correlation between age and these statistics. Young people are just as likely to be strong supporters of Catholic schools as older people. My colleague, William McCready, has estimated that over 1.8 billion dollars is available in untapped support for Catholics schools; and my colleague, Kathleen McCourt, has demonstrated that two thirds of the decline in Catholic school enrollment during the last ten years is attributable to the failure of church administrators to build new schools.

A good operational definition of the communal Catholic might be that he is someone who does not go to church every week, but still wants his children to go to Catholic schools and is willing to contribute more money to keep the schools going. Not all communal Catholics fall under this rubric, of course, and not all under it would fit the communal Catholic definition on other criteria. But the communal Catholic has not the slightest doubt about the continuation of

Catholic schools. He cannot understand why both the hierarchy and the "intellectuals" have given up on the schools.

In a certain city there are three Catholic schools. St. Athanasius is a battered old building, sitting on a grimy street where every third car is a police patrol. It is in the middle of the poorest neighborhood in the city, a neighborhood gradually being abandoned by all but its most destitute black inhabitants. From the outside, St. Athanasius looks as if it is about to be abandoned too, but inside, its classrooms are brightly painted, gaily decorated, and filled with students. Its multiracial faculty teaches to full classrooms. Despite the poverty of the neighborhood, the parish school board of parents (all black) has set the tuition at $500 a year per child, $650 per family. St. Athanasius loses money each year, but not very much. Of its $80,000 a year budget, $76,000 comes from tuition. (And not all the charged tuition is collected.) The heat and the light in the school are subsidized by the Sunday collection in the parish, although the fifty churchgoers who appear in the gloom of the great, gray Romanesque church each Sunday do not contribute much because they do not have very much. The overwhelming majority of the students in St. Athanasius are not Catholic, of course.

Holy Sepulchre is set in one of the most affluent neighborhoods in the city amid tree lined streets and rolling hills. It has a contemporary style church and a school with twenty classrooms. The old basketball court has been filled with nine portable classrooms. Only four of the thirty teachers are nuns; the rest are lay people with salaries comparable to those of the public school teachers who work across the street. (This salary scale has been decreed by the school board, which is made up of successful business and professional men and their wives.) The school board permits no more than thirty students in a classroom and has a waiting list of applicants. The tuition is slightly higher than that of St. Athanasius, but the crowds of Catholics who swarm into Holy Sepulchre church on Sunday morning contribute a huge subsidy (best guess: $50,000 a year) to the school from their Sunday contributions. All would be well at Holy

Sepulchre if parishioners did not fear the black ghetto only a little more than a half mile away. How long the church will be full on Sunday remains to be seen.

St. Fabiola is in the midst of one of the raw, new, working, and lower-middle-class suburbs on the fringe of the city. As one bumps down the rutted, unpaved street by the tiny bungalows and the low sprawling building attached to the church, it looks just like any other parochial school. Yet, St. Fabiola has no parochial school. The two nuns who are assigned at the parish wear lay garb and are listed on the masthead of the parish paper as members of the team equal to the pastor and his curate. They preside over a "religious education" program carried on in the classrooms of the "school," but the religious education program is not a parochial school. There are classes for adults, teenagers, and elementary school children given in the afternoons, evenings, and on weekends. The costs of building and maintaining a parochial school enterprise at St. Fabiola's were deemed much too high. The pastor, with the approval of the archbishop, decided not to try the parochial school route. Attendance at the religious education programs is good, though perhaps only half the children of the parish show up—about as many, the pastor ruefully remarks, as would have gone to a parochial school if there were one. Whether the people of the parish are satisfied with this compromise is not clear; no one ever bothered to ask them.

St. Athanasius, Holy Sepulchre, St. Fabiola—here in brief image is the story of Catholic education in the United States. Unsung alternative education in the inner city, flourishing parochial school in an affluent parish, and abandonment of the parochial school tradition in a suburb where there seems to be little money and less will to continue the tradition. Are parochial schools in trouble then? The black parents of St. Athanasius hardly think so. They maintain their own private school out of tuition with a small financial subsidy from the parish and the personal investment of the lives of the priests and the nuns who teach there. Nor are the parents in Holy Sepulchre particularly aware of the crisis. Their school is expensive, but in their judgment it is worth the cost. If they can hold their community together they will continue to provide religious education as well as general education for their children. Indeed, many of the younger parents of the parish graduated from Holy Sepulchre themselves and have moved back into the neighborhood to raise their own children with the advantages they enjoyed. (From inside the Irish Catholic ghetto it does look like an advantage to be there.) As for the Catholics of St. Fabiola, the parochial school crisis has come and gone. For them parochial schools are part of the past.

That there is a crisis in parochial schools is beyond doubt. In 1967, there were slightly over five million students in Catholic schools; now, there are a little over four million. In 1967, there were almost thirteen thousand schools; there are now less than eleven thousand. In 1960, about one-quarter of the teachers on the staffs of parochial elementary schools were lay (only seven percent in 1950); now, lay faculty is approaching the three-fifths mark. More than eighty percent of the parochial elementary schools in the country charge less than $200 a year tuition per student, while in 1972 per pupil cost of the Catholic school was $268 and going up at a rate in excess of 10 percent a year. The President's Panel on Nonpublic Education estimates that between 1970 and 1980, seven states (California, Illinois, Michigan, Ohio, Pennsylvania, New York, and New Jersey) will lose an enrollment in nonpublic schools of over one and a half million. Almost all this loss is in Catholic schools, of course. When Peter Rossi and I did our study of the effects of Catholic education in the early 1960s, we estimated that more than two fifths of school age Catholics in the country were in parochial elementary schools. The figure at the present time must be closer to one third.

The conventional wisdom inside and outside the church is that decline in enrollment is the result of a mixture of increased costs and disenchantment of Catholic parents. In the church after the Vatican Council, it is argued, the relevance of parochial schools is no longer so obvious to large numbers of Catholic parents. Yet in survey after survey over the last twenty years, a little more than two thirds of the

Catholic population has indicated support for parochial schools. There is no evidence in the survey data that this proportion has diminished at all. Unquestionably, some Catholic parents have pulled their children out of parochial schools because this is the enlightened and progressive thing to do. Undoubtedly, other parents have not sent their children to parochial schools because the costs are too high.

Yet, in fact, much of the decline in parochial school enrollment is the result of the closing of uneconomic schools and the failure to build new schools. The Catholic population continues to move from the central city to the suburbs. In the 1940s and 1950s, parochial school construction kept pace with this movement; in the 1960s, there was relatively little new school construction. How much the failure to build new schools where the Catholic population is moving has affected the decline in enrollment is difficult to determine. Catholic school administrators have only slight interest in data collection or high quality research. But there is little reason to doubt that the construction of new schools has diminished drastically, and this is an important factor in explaining the enrollment decline. Furthermore, insofar as there is any evidence, parents oppose the closing of the old school, and whenever anyone bothers to consult them they vigorously support construction of a new one.

Could St. Fabiola have supported a parochial school? If St. Athanasius can, surely St. Fabiola could. Did the parents of St. Fabiola want a school? No one knows, because no one bothered to find out. Should a parochial school have been built at St. Fabiola? The pastor and the bishop decided that it shouldn't, which may well have been the proper decision. But the point is worth emphasizing. The St. Fabiola decision was based neither on lay disenchantment nor a clear absence of funds; it was made by ecclesiastical administrators who decided that they did not want a parochial school at St. Fabiola. It is neither finances nor waning popularity, then, that will put parochial schools out of business. One of the most able Catholic educators, Bishop William McManus of Chicago, has commented that the threat does not come from "monetary difficulties, nor declining enrollment, nor a diminished number of religious on the faculty." On the contrary, the parochial school system is committing suicide.

To understand this self-destruction, one must grasp what a powerful symbolic issue parochial schools have always been in the history of the United States. Indeed, the symbolism swirling around the parochial schools is so powerful that anyone who tries to write about the subject in categories that have not been hallowed by the century-long debate is likely to find himself clobbered by both sides. Neither the friends nor the enemies of parochial schools want dispassion and objectivity. The parochial schools were begun in this country as a Catholic response to a perceived threat from nativist bigotry. Only in their own school system, it was said, would Catholic children be free from the proselytizing efforts of the public schools, which were then in fact nondenominational Protestant schools. On the other hand, the native Americans used the parochial schools as evidence that Catholics did not want to become really American, and that they intended to maintain a loyalty to a foreign power. A few parochial schools were burned and many exposes were written about the terrible things that went on within them. Even today, an occasional Protestant organization will issue a statement claiming that parochial schools are a haven for racists who do not want to go to racially integrated white schools.

The assumption that somehow Catholic schools are unAmerican is still strong in the American Protestant and sometimes, the Jewish collective subconscious. The United States is virtually the only country in the Western world that does not provide some sort of state aid for parochial schools. Chief Justice Burger's "entanglement" doctrine that purports to protect states from getting "messed up" in religious problems by supporting Catholic schools may be bad law and bad sociology, but it is good history. The American national consensus has never approved parochial schools; it has only tolerated them. While the consensus may have become more sympathetic, it only follows that there is a bit more tolerance. Most non-Catholic Americans, especially most public education administrators, would be delighted to see the parochial schools go away—although they would not want it to happen within their own school districts, because their schools might then be inundated with Catholic students.

There is now enough research evidence to refute the hoary myths about the deficiencies of Catholic education. It is now reasonably well known that the whole day is not spent in the Catholic classroom working on religious indoctrination with a bit of spelling just before recess. Nor does the half hour a day religious instruction necessarily impede efficiency in other educational activities. Nevertheless many public educators and some progressive Catholics are reluctant to concede that parochial schools are on the whole as good as if not a little better than the American educational average.

Despite crowded classrooms and so-called inadequate teacher-training, students in the Catholic schools do at least as well as if not better than students in comparable public schools on standardized tests. In one diocese, for example, seventh graders are six tenths of a year ahead of the national average in reading, seven tenths of a year ahead in language skills, and six tenths of a year ahead in math skills. There is considerable disagreement as to how much difference a school makes in scores on standardized achievement tests, but there is no evidence that students in parochial schools are at all educationally handicapped. (The black students in the St. Athanasius school are two grades ahead in achievement over students in the neighboring public school.)

Parochial school graduates do even better in the social and economic race than Catholics who went to public schools. They are also more enlightened on questions of race and social policy. But myths rarely yield to data, and the suspicions about and fear of Catholic schools are still powerful in the land. Wouldn't it be better, the American consensus asks, for Catholics to go to the same schools as everyone else? Or, as one Protestant churchman put it in the wake of the Vatican Council, ought not Catholics now abandon their own schools and go to the "American schools" like everyone else?

Nativist opposition to Catholic schools is not new, of course. What is new is that a substantial proportion of the Catholic-educated are willing to buy the traditional non-Catholic view of the parochial schools. This phenomenon can only be understood as part of the rapid acculturation into American society that has occurred among Catholic ethnic groups since the end of World War II.

When a group you perceive as oppressive identifies a particular institution with your cause, then, far from giving that institution up, you rally to its support. British oppression in Ireland guaranteed the identification of Catholicism with Irish nationalism. To be a good Irishman you had to be a loyal Catholic. Similarly, the Catholic church flourishes in Poland today because Catholicism is a way of asserting one's Polishness in the face of a regime dominated by a foreign power. Precisely because the parochial schools were a prime target for native American attack (attacks that the Catholics thought represented bigotry), the Catholic population rallied to enthusiastic support of the parochial schools. To a very considerable extent the American Catholic church became an educational institution, putting vast quantities of time, money, and personnel into supporting the most extensive private school system in the world. The emergence of the separate Catholic school system in the United States has to be seen as one phase in the acculturation of the ethnic immigrant groups—the phase of militant defensiveness.

Late in the last century, however, that small group of Catholics who had managed to break out of the immigrant environment to receive some kind of tentative acceptance in the larger society became critical of the Catholic schools. When they perceived the Catholic school from outside the ghetto, the school did indeed begin to look divisive and un-American. Whether the Catholic critics of parochial schools were turncoats who had sold out to the enemy or progressive pioneers depended on one's perspective; but as long as they were a minority and did not have much impact on the Catholic educators themselves, they were no real threat. But since World War II, American Catholics have moved rapidly into the upper-middle class. Priests and religious who teach in the Catholic schools are often now the sons and daughters of college-educated parents. They may have done graduate work in non-Catholic colleges and universities. If they are on the faculties of Catholic higher education institutions and are under forty, they almost certainly did graduate work in non-Catholic universities. Many of the editors and authors of the most influential Catholic journals like *Commonweal* and the *National Catholic Reporter* are ashamed of and angry at the immigrant ghetto parishes of their childhoods. The quintessential symbol of all that was wrong with that ghetto parish is the parochial school that stood at its core.

The new Catholic intelligentsia, then, is almost unanimously against a separate Catholic school system (even when it earns its support from that system). Given the general absence of serious scholarship within Catholic education, the intelligentsia has carried the day almost without opposition. Few Catholic educators today will not concede in private conversation that they no longer have much confidence in what they are doing. The Catholic school system was not prepared intellectually or emotionally for the dramatic change in social and economic status in the Catholic population. Nor was it prepared for the emergence of an anticlerical and antiparochial school intellectual elite. The morale of Catholic educators collapsed almost overnight. Indeed, one book, Mary Perkins Ryan's *Are Parochial Schools the Answer?*, published in the early 1960s, came as a death blow to the confidence of Catholic educators. That one book could topple the edifice is good evidence that the mortar was crumbling to begin with.

The trauma of the Vatican Council II was another severe blow to Catholic educators. Most of them (perhaps I should say, most of us) were raised in an atmosphere of certainties—religious, moral, ecclesiastical, and liturgical. Without warning, the turmoil unleashed by the Council destroyed most of these certainties. All the rigid structural supports of our commitments and convictions were swept away, and for the first time in our lives we had to face fundamental questions of meaning and vocation that had been either repressed or had never arisen. We found ourselves asking whether we believed anything any more and whether what we were doing was worth anything. American Catholicism was simply not equipped to answer these questions. And while some of us managed to survive, for better or worse, others experienced acute and painful personality disorientation. Priests and nuns left their vocations by the thousands. Religious communities tore themselves apart in internal conflict in which the liberals usually won the field, only to leave it. Still others decided that they would do anything but be bogged down in the foolishness of the Catholic school system: run for Congress, write speeches for Nixon, plot make-believe revolutions, design sets, take up modern dance, be a sociologist even—anything to be relevant.

Who wanted to spend days in a classroom with a bunch of snotty kids? Even the more conservative clergy who had risen to the rank of pastor in Catholic parishes were not so sure any more. On the one hand they would extol the merits of Catholic schools, and on the other they would hesitate about taking on the huge debt necessary to build such schools and maintain them. Catholic education administrators would go to meetings of their teachers and preach confidence and optimism, then go back to their offices and sign letters closing an uneconomical high school. And bishops would issue solemn proclamations of commitment to Catholic education but discourage the building of new parochial schools in the suburbs.

It was no longer clear, then, to the leadership of Catholic school education, or to the ordinary rank and file teachers, that the separate school system was worth the cost. The number of lay teachers was increasing, salaries for teachers were going up, construction costs were skyrocketing. None of these were insurmountable problems for people who believed unquestioningly in what they were doing. But it was no longer possible to believe that way. Catholic educators were no longer convinced that parochial schools were necessary.

In the theoretical desert created by this collapse of confidence, all sorts of strange plants began to flourish. Sensitivity training, encounter sessions, Pentecostalism, ecumenism that virtually denied religious differences, yoga, intimate relationships between priests and nuns (sometimes sexless, sometimes not), radical militancy (despite the fact that many black parents were anything but enthusiastic about such militancy for *their* children), celebration of the joys of the "secular city," brave announcements that God was dead (which most parochial school children accepted as indifferently as they had the announcement that the Blessed Mother had appeared in the Philippine Islands), and self-defined counterculture liturgies—all of these have made the current parochial school scene a fascinating area for anthropological research. The natives are restless indeed.

Catholic higher educational institutions have been acutely embarrassed by the fact that they are enrolling a smaller proportion of Catholics each year. Never mind that Catholic attendance at colleges has generally increased dramatically in the last two decades. (In 1960, twenty-five percent of the college students in the country were Catholic, which is about the same proportion as in the national population; in 1972, thirty-three percent of the college students were Catholic.) Never mind that most Catholic colleges have been able to maintain their enrollments in the face of the current enrollment crisis. Even a decline in relative proportion was enough to lead Catholic college administrators to wrestle with the question: What is a Catholic college? Once such a question is asked and taken seriously, there is no way to answer it without defining many of the things that the college is engaged in. The latent assumption in this question is that there isn't any difference between a Catholic college and any other kind of college. Such an assertion is a historical and sociological absurdity, but Catholic intellectuals are not well known for letting reality get in the way of their ideas. Hence, the fashion of Catholic higher education in the 1960s was to become as much like everyone else and as quickly as possible. Every Catholic institution seemed to have a comparable non-Catholic school that became its model. One was told that a given college was a "Catholic Carleton" or a

"Catholic Emory" or a "Catholic Amherst" or—heaven save us—
that Notre Dame was on its way to becoming a "Catholic Princeton." It did not occur to many educators that if they became like
everyone else, they would have nothing unique to offer, and that parents might well decide to send their children to the real Carleton,
Amherst, Emory, or Princeton.

A certain Catholic college I know of had a long and glorious history of providing college educations for young women from
working-class ethnic families. There was even research evidence that
this school had considerable social and psychological impact on the
young teachers it was training. But in the middle 1960s (while it was
still searching dormitory rooms and confiscating whiskey bottles
from students, incidentally) this college decided that it would become a secular and ecumenical college. It proclaimed in a series of
national magazine ads how relevant it was and how much it was
"with" all the trends. Now it finds itself in the peculiar position of
trying to discover whether it has anything unique to offer. Ethnic
parents are asking in effect, "If you are no different from anyone
else, why should we pay good money to send our daughters to your
school?" A fair question.

The fundamental crisis in Catholic schools is neither financial nor
organizational; it is theoretical. They will not be routed by external
foes, increasing costs, apathetic laity, or Supreme Court decisions
that are faithful to nativist tradition in denying tax support. Catholic
schools will go out of existence mostly because Catholic educators
no longer have enough confidence in what they are doing to sustain
the momentum and the sacrifice that built the world's largest private
school system. The Holy See and the bishops issue periodic pronouncements about the importance of Catholic schools but is it to be
feared that no one is listening. Both the pope and the bishops have
long since lost their credibility. Scarcely a kind word has been spo-
ken in favor of the parochial schools by the Catholic intelligentsia.
And those of us who have assayed a kind adjective or two have been
ignored.

Paradoxically, administrative techniques, record keeping, effective teaching, educational innovation, even research have all improved dramatically in the Catholic Schools. Even non-Catholic educators are willing to say that the performance of Catholic Schools is now at an all time high, and some educators like Donald Ericson of the University of Chicago are vigorous in their support for all non-public schools.

Yet morale is still low. One of the nuns who teaches at St. Athanasius remarked to me, "We're not really reaching the people here that we should be reaching." I was astonished, for it seemed to me that she and her colleagues were teaching precisely those children who would have a very hard time making it out of poverty without St. Athanasius. But she was not satisfied. "The kids we get," she said, "are those whose parents are interested in their getting a good education. We are missing completely those whose parents are indifferent." I suppose sister was right. (In grammar school I learned that sister was always right.) St. Athanasius is indeed educating those poor black children who are educable by our current educational technology. She wanted to give them up to try to educate those with whom she could make little if any progress. There may well be some special kind of religious zeal in such a desire for failure, a zeal that can overlook the importance of a critical work that no one else is doing. My guess is that it is rather a manifestation of what Father Edward Duff called "the mass masochism" of a group that is in the last stages of winning full acceptance in the larger American society.

What are the prospects for the future? There is, of course, massive dissatisfaction with the failures of public education. As Colin Greer has recently pointed out in his book, *The Great School Legend,* black immigrants to the city are only the most recent immigrant groups the public school has failed to serve. (Why Greer, an able, careful, and responsible researcher, ignores the work of the parochial school among previous generations of immigrants as well as among today's blacks is a puzzle.) That public education has failed in the great cities of the country is now hardly a matter of debate. It is also clear that every extra dollar poured into urban public education would be absorbed into the teachers' salaries now demanded by the militant unions and will have little if any impact on what happens to a student in the classroom. Despite the immense power of the public education establishment, talk about breaking its monopoly is growing more vigorous even in those enlightened liberal circles where public education has always found its strongest support. "Competition," "pluralism," and "open marketplace" are catchwords one hears more and more frequently. Indeed, one suspects that enthusiasm for nonpublic schools would have been much more powerful if someone had thought of a way to subsidize private schools without subsidizing Catholic schools. In a way, the existence of ten thousand parochial schools is one of the last strongholds protecting the public education bureaucracy from its liberal critics. For the public educator can always point to the parochial school and say to the liberal or radical critic, "But do you really want to give money to them?"

Furthermore, there is increasing support for a constitutionally sound means of state and federal support for nonpublic schools. *The New Republic* broke with the liberal party line a number of years ago and endorsed such a notion. More recently, Adam Walinski, writing in that journal, strongly urged tax credit support for Catholic schools. He went so far as to suggest that opposition to such aid among the liberal elites was fundamentally anti-Catholic. The President's Panel on Nonpublic Education has suggested tax credits, construction loan programs, tuition reimbursement, and voucher experiments as means of facilitating the work of nonpublic schools. A climate of opinion, then, is beginning to develop that is both skeptical of the public education monopoly and sympathetic to the search for constitutional means to support private schools, including religious ones.

But opposition to such aid is still vigorous. Both public educators and Protestant, Jewish, and secularist pressure groups argue that such aid is completely foreign to the American tradition of separation of church and state—and it surely is foreign to that interpretation of the Constitution that has held sway for the last several decades. Judging the temper of the Supreme Court from its recent decisions, one might be tempted to conclude that the court will strike down any system of aid to Catholic schools no matter how sound the constitutional argument is in its favor. Presidential candidates, of course, will continue to endorse such aid as a matter of general principle, and then not do much about it in practical legislation.

At the present reading, the prospects for governmental aid (either state or federal) for Catholic schools must be considered unlikely. Such aid would not solve the problems of morale and theory, but it might create a breathing space in which such problems could be more reasonably faced. In the present atmosphere of panic, the only real attention to the problems of theory and morale are frantic exhortations from bishops and school superintendents.

What will happen if Catholic schools do vanish? The Catholic church will doubtless survive; so will urban public education, although there will be a huge increase in enrollment in public schools in many cities and still more of an educational tax drain. Whether the whole of American society will suffer because of the loss of the largest alternative to the public educational monopoly that currently exists depends on whether you think alternative education ought to be available.

Christopher Jencks, et al., believe in maximizing freedom of educational opportunities. But what if Jencks's suggestions were followed and every school open to all were declared to be a "public school," deserving of tax support? Would there not be then a proliferation of private schools, many of them also religious in orientation? There may be an increase in non-Catholic parochial schools (though American Protestantism has not been enthusiastic in the past about developing its own school systems, with the notable exception of the Lutheran Church Missouri Synod). If you believe that a wide range of educational choice is a bad thing for American society, you will be appalled by the thought of an increase in non-Catholic parochial schools and delighted at the prospect of trouble for Catholic schools. If, on the other hand, you believe in an open educational marketplace, you are scarcely likely to be happy about the demise of public education's only serious competition—particularly when that competition is present in the worst inner-city slums.

The circumstances being as they are, only the most naive would attempt prophecy. One therefore hedges the bet: The parochial schools will survive, but they will be different. They will play a different role in the future than they did in the past. For this sort of prediction, you don't win Pulitzer prizes.

It is appropriate to end with St. Athanasius, whose dirty red bricks cut off what little sunlight the steelmill pollution might permit into my room. At this time, in the archdiocese of Chicago, the church provides almost three million dollars of subsidy a year to forty-five inner-city schools with more than thirty thousand students, only two fifths of whom are Catholic. Black people make up a total of about 1.8 percent of the U.S. Catholic population; they constitute 5.1 percent of the students in Catholic elementary schools, and 3.7 percent of the students in Catholic high schools. It is a safe guess, then, that more than half of the blacks in parochial schools are not Catholic. Surely in St. Athanasius the overwhelming majority are not Catholic. St. Athanasius is an ecumenical private school controlled by a school board of black parents, providing alternative education in one of the poorest neighborhoods in the city. The church provides a small financial subsidy (although in some inner city parishes the diocesan subsidy can be over $200,000 a year). The largest subsidy comes from the life commitment of a group of priests and nuns. I trust I shall be excused from observing that efforts like St. Athanasius represent not only the finest hour of the Catholic school system but one of the finest things in American Catholicism.

The inner city alternative Catholic school may have come into being unintentionally, even unconsciously. The Catholic church itself seems only vaguely aware that places like St. Athanasius are doing anything relevant. No one has suggested that the results of Chief Justice Burger's fears of "entanglement" may ultimately put

St. Athanasius out of business. Catholic liberals and non-Catholic critics don't care and pay little attention to St. Athanasius. And the mass media, so interested in the problems of the city, are apparently unaware of its existence too.

About the only ones who give a damn about St. Athanasius are the parents of the children who attend it. If the Catholic schools do eventually disappear from the land, the highest price of all will be paid by the parents and children of St. Athanasius. But they are only black "respectables," and nobody cares much about them.

The reader can refer to *Catholic Schools in a Changing Church* for details of the statistical data which support the position taken in this chapter. To summarize them briefly:

1. Support for Catholic schools among the Catholic laity has not wavered one bit since 1963. On the contrary, the schools seem to be the only institution in the church to have been unaffected by the ecumenical disasters of the last decade.

2. Support for the schools is as strong among the laity in their twenties as among those in their sixties.

3. Catholic schools do have a notable impact—independent of the religiousness of parents—on the adult religious behavior of those who attended such schools. This impact has not been adversely affected by the changes of the last decade.

4. Those who attended Catholic schools were more likely to support the Vatican Council changes than those who did not.

5. The reason for the decline in parochial school enrollment is apparently almost entirely the result of the failure to construct new schools.

6. Catholic education correlates positively with progressive attitudes on race.

CHAPTER TWELVE

A Church for the Communal Catholic

The communal Catholic, I have argued in this book, is committed to Catholicism as a community of Americans, and to the Catholic symbol system—often in an inarticulate and unexplicit fashion, but not to the organizational structure of the American church. He is not angry at the church, not disillusioned about it, not in revolt against it. He has pleasant memories of the church of his childhood, but he simply does not find the church in its official leadership or its unofficial intelligentsia to be credible as a teacher of human behavior.

Almost necessarily, then, the communal Catholic must cope with the problems and the resources of the present moment by himself. There is no one to whom he can turn for information about heritage or tradition or theory; no one with whom he can ally himself against the romantics and the nativists. His support for neighborhoods, for pluralism, and for parochial schools, his sympathy for the ethnic revival, his hunches about the Catholic view of the nature of human nature, and his perception of the possibilities in the present religious situation are all essentially individualistic. The communal Catholic is skeptical of all organizations, especially religious organizations. He doesn't necessarily like his present isolated position, and would like community as well as communalism. He may occasionally talk about religion with other people of like mind; he may even be an active member of his parish—for want of something better—but he has no illusion that the parish can or will respond to his religious needs. He remains a religious individualist despite himself.

My own disposition is to fault the communal Catholic for this individualism which is against the very tradition which he claims to value. On the other hand, given the present state of the American church, I cannot blame him too much; and if he argues that the American church in its present state is beyond reform, I can only say, as one who has knocked his head against the brick wall for a long time,* that he may well be right.

Still, the communal Catholic needs a church. He would perhaps be the first to admit it.

A church for the communal Catholic would be nothing more than an ecclesial institution which has regained its credibility, one the communal Catholic would turn to for more than just sacramental ministry. To ask how one can build a church for the communal Catholic is merely to ask how the church in the United States can recapture its credibility.

Let me set down schematically the definition of "communal Catholic."

1. The communal Catholic is loyal to Catholicism. It is his religious self-definition. He will have no other.

2. The communal Catholic is not angry at the ecclesiastical structure.

3. He does not expect to receive important instruction from that structure on any issue, ranging from sexuality to international economics.

4. Nevertheless, he is interested in and fascinated by the Catholic

---

*As I write this page, the Chicago press carries an account of our brilliant cardinal objecting to the National Labor Relations Board calling a collective bargaining election for the teachers (many of them lay) at the diocesan seminaries. This, he tells us, is government interference in church affairs. The church apparently is immune to the provisions of the National Labor Relations Act. The same cardinal is of course appalled when the courts rule that aid to parochial schools is "entangling" the state in church affairs. And he's too dumb to perceive the contradiction.

tradition to which he is loyal, and wishes to understand it better.

5. The communal Catholic seeks sacramental ministry from the church at such times in his life when such ministry seems appropriate and necessary—for some, every day, for others, only at rites of passage like baptism, marriage, and death.

Three of the above characteristics have been with us almost since the beginning of American Catholicism. We have always had Catholics who refused to take the teaching authority seriously and who reserved the right to determine for themselves when they needed sacramental ministry, while remaining loyal to the church. The encouraging aspect of the tremendous increase in the numbers of communal Catholics is that it is still possible for the institutional church to talk to them because they are interested in the Catholic tradition and are not angry at the institutional church. These qualities are new elements in the new breed of communal Catholics. (The result is that some communal Catholics may fall closer to daily sacramental ministry than at any time in the past.) They are, in fact, quite proud of being Catholic.

David Tracy describes the style and concern of communal Catholics:

. . . there has recently emerged in American culture a new social reality: persons unmistakably Catholic in their sensibilities and outlooks, yet seemingly uninterested in most central institutional and . . . most "internal" questions of the Catholic heritage. This increasingly influential (because largely professional) social group seem able to recognize the fact that, in spite of their lack of interest in officially Catholic issues, they find themselves irretrievably Catholic. Their approach to social, political and professional issues, their hopes for and vision of the good society, their sensibilities and desires, their most cherished hopes and most articulate self-understandings—in a word, what I have called their "ethos"—can only be named "Catholic."*

What is basically happening, it seems, is that the "communal

---

*An unpublished article by David Tracy, "Reflections on Communal Catholicism."

Catholics" have opted out (not necessarily "copped out") of the more strictly internal concerns of institutional Catholicism in favor of retrieving certain central features of the Catholic sensibility. They seem, for example, more interested in symbol and story than in dogma; more concerned to appropriate the richness of "tradition" than to debate upon the relative merits of various "tradita"; more committed to what can only be called a radically "incarnational" or "sacramental" Catholic vision of reality even if less interested in understanding that vision in explicitly "incarnational" or "sacramental" terms; more intrigued by a Catholic sensibility dimension to our common lives than by bringing that sensibility to bear upon explicitly or, at least, instantly recognizable "Catholic" concerns; more resonant, perhaps, to the sensibilities of a George Santayana than of an Orestes Brownson; more alive to the experiences of an F. Scott Fitzgerald than of an Evelyn Waugh; more intrigued by the real difficulties of Graham Greenes's *The Honorary Consul* than by the mysterious comings and goings in *The Heart of the Matter*.

The institutional church is not listened to because the communal Catholic, regretfully but not angrily, has concluded that the church doesn't know what it is talking about. The principal cause of the decline in credibility, of course, is sex. As is demonstrated in *Catholic Schools in a Changing Church,* the principal cause of the catastrophic decline in American Catholicism in the last decade and a half was not the Vatican Council but the encyclical letter, *Humanae Vitae.** It is idle to speculate what course communal Catholics would have taken had it not been for *Humanae Vitae,* for the encyclical affected not only the credibility of the church as sexual teacher but the credibility of the church as teacher in any area.

Thus in the NORC study we see that Catholics have become much more enlightened on racial issues than they were ten years ago, but they are now less likely to concede the right of the church to teach on

---

*Note, however, that even here the communal Catholic is selective. He is, for example, generally loyal to the church's traditional teaching on abortion. He continues to believe it is wrong even though he may hesitate to impose his convictions on those who do not share his on this matter.

matters of race—a finding which will seem paradoxical only if one expects changes in Catholic racial attitudes to be the *result* of the church's teaching. Catholics are saying in effect that they are more tolerant racially not *because* of what the church has said and not *in spite of* what the church has said, but quite independently of either. They are telling the church "We have become more tolerant, but not because you have told us to be more tolerant."

It is also interesting to note that the precipitous decline among Catholics in the conviction that religion has an important influence on American life is much sharper than a comparable decline among American Protestants, and occurred entirely *after* the issuance of the birth control encyclical. At the very time when clergy, religious, and ecclesiastical administrators were doing all in their power to become more "relevant," they were in fact becoming much less so. Indeed it is very likely that the attempt to acquire relevance, by giving specific concrete answers to specific social and moral problems, contributed substantially to the decline in credibility. The church didn't know what it was talking about on sexuality—or so it seemed to most Catholics—and then it began to pontificate about politics and international economics, which it did not seem to know much about either. Why bother to listen?

It is consoling for ecclesiastical leaders to think that such rejection of official teaching is a manifestation of selfishness or materialism (as the American bishops argued in their report to the international synod in 1974), but there is little evidence to substantiate such an argument. It also may be consoling to some members of the Catholic left to argue that the church's failure to take a stand on such issues as war, race, and international economics has cost it its credibility. In fact, however, it is precisely the acceptance of the right to take such stands that has declined in the last decade. Most communal Catholics are neither "leftists" nor "rightists" but part of the moderate and generous American political majority. They will listen to the church, of course, when it speaks on sexuality, race, or international problems, but they will listen seriously only when the church has established first that it knows what it is talking about. To summarize the challenge of communal Catholicism to the ecclesial institution in a single sentence: communal Catholics will no longer accept what the church says on social and moral issues merely because the church has said it. Indeed, until the church manages to reassert its credibility they will barely listen to it when it speaks.

The ecclesial institution will recapture its credibility with the communal Catholics when it begins to acquire the characteristics described in the following six seeming paradoxes:

1. It must be both *humble* and *excellent*.
2. It must be both *traditional* and *radical*.
3. It must be both *relaxed* and *committed*.
4. It must be both *intellectual* and *sensitive*.
5. It must be both *realistic* and *hopeful*.
6. It must be both *mature* and *enthusiastic*.

It is part of the problem of our time that the qualities in each of the above pairs seem paradoxical if not contradictory. In other ages they would have seemed complementary.

A humble church is free to admit that it doesn't have all the answers. Ecclesiastical authority would feel under no constraint to provide specific solutions to all the dilemmas of human sexuality, for example. Catholic social actionists would also be free to acknowledge that they do not have all the answers to problems of poverty and injustice. Both the Catholic left and the Catholic right presently seem to assume that if you are Catholic you have to be certain. The admission of hesitancy, doubt, or uncertainty is somehow or other a violation of the Catholic faith. It is understandable that such an assumption would be made given the events of the past several hundred years. How else could one resist the certainties of the Enlightenment save with one's own certainties? But the Enlightenment is dead now, and we no longer need to respond to its arrogance with an arrogance of our own. We are certain of one thing only: the love of God as it has been revealed in Jesus. The temptation to transfer that certainty to all other matters under heaven has been a strong one throughout the history of Christendom. It is a temptation to idolatry, to absolutize the relative, to make necessary the contingent. The best eras in the history of the church are those when the temptation was resisted.*

A humble church is not necessarily a relativistic one. It does matter what you believe; not all positions are of equal merit and not everything everyone says is true. But the church states its own position with the full realization—and its long history certainly reinforces it—that no single position on any moral or social issue can contain the *whole* truth; and that its own position will grow, develop, and refine itself as its understanding becomes deeper and richer. Truth, the humble church will insist, is absolute and relative, but the ways in which poor humans try to state the truth are indeed very relative, and always bound by the circumstances of time and place in which we find ourselves.

But because the church is tentative and humble, it does not thereby become indifferent or slipshod. Because it realizes that stands on moral and social issues are always limited and inadequate, it does not dispense itself from a passion for excellence. The Lord grants the increase, but that does not mean that Paul is excused from a competent job of planting or Apollo from a skillful job of watering. Communal Catholics, for the most part, are professional, and they expect the same professionalism from their church. At preaching and teaching it should be competent in both substance and style. A papacy or a national hierarchy, giving detailed advice on almost every conceivable social and moral issue, will find it very difficult to do what is most important for it to do: to illumine the fundamental meaning of human life and death. Similarly, a parish priest who tries to be a jack-of-all-trades—from a psychiatric counselor to a community organizer—is likely to turn out to be bad at preaching the Word of God, which is the most important thing he does. The communal Catholics I know are unanimous on one point: most priests are terrible preachers.**

*St. Thomas points out that there is only one object of faith: God. Faith, he says, is one, not only in the act by which we believe but also in the object in which we believe.

**An opinion strongly supported by the rest of the American Catholic population, as the research evidence demonstrates.

Gregorian chants may no longer be sung in church, but you see record albums of them in the homes of many communal Catholics. Ecclesial Catholics may be ashamed of their immigrant roots and contemptuous of the old neighborhood; communal Catholics are fascinated by them. Mariology may be completely out of fashion in the church; the communal Catholic wonders how a cultural symbol which dominated the Western world for fifteen hundred years could possibly be out of fashion. Chesterton may be the laughing stock of the ecclesials, but the communal Catholic finds his essays delightful. Newman, Aquinas, Teresa of Avila, Hopkins, Augustine, John of the Cross—all of these giants of the preconciliar years are people of interest to many communal Catholics, not because they appeal to sentimental nostalgia but because they represent a heritage and a tradition which the communal Catholic realizes has shaped him. He does not want to become encapsulated by tradition, as we were in the pre-Vatican church; he does not want to return to anything, he is not interested in turning the clock back; but neither does he believe that the past can be dismissed simply as irrelevant or old fashioned. The truths and the symbols which served humankind for a millenium and a half may conceivably still have something to say to us. He may be very inarticulate and confused in his own mind about all of this, but he knows that while he does not want to go back to the past, he would nevertheless like to carry the best of the past forward with him into the doubts and uncertainties of the future.

But if the church of the communal Catholic must be traditional, it also must be radical—which is not necessarily the same thing as saying that it must be leftist. What passes for radicalism today is often not very radical at all. In substance the so-called Catholic radicalism is often nothing more than radical chic—the fashionable cliches of the university and the mass media. In style it is often a mixture of anger, guilt, apocalypse, and rudeness. In terms of personnel it is usually made up of people who do little more than take stands and issue statements. In its base it is establishmentarian, since it draws its membership from church bureaucracies, the mass media, and the academy. The so-called Catholic left usually proposes to do little more than replace the large corporate bureaucracies of the capitalist state with the large corporate bureaucracies of the socialist state.

The romantic radicalism of Ivan Illich at least avoids *that* mistake, although his critique of corporate bureaucracy does not point the way to any alternative which would not demand the dismantling of industrial society. The real radical challenge of our time is to find ways to build social structures which can combine the productivity of the industrial corporation with the warmth and support of the peasant village. Equality with freedom and independence with communal responsibility are part of the tradition of Catholicism. There can be a unique contribution out of the Catholic tradition in the search for a more just and human society. To be more authentically radical, the church must search its own experience for a critique of the present social structures that is something more than just a repetition of other people's critiques and more than a proposal to substitute one form of large corporate bureaucratic oppression for another. Capitalist bureaucracies are not very efficient, but they are more so than socialist bureaucracies, it would seem. They are also apparently no less humane. But the communal Catholic will not be interested in listening to a church which proposes alternatives that someone else is already proposing. He will wonder why a world view as unique as the Catholic world view, and a tradition with as much experience as the Catholic tradition has nothing of its own to contribute.

One need not turn to quotations from papal encyclicals or the Chester-Belloc distributism to look for ideas. Of all the multinational institutions in the world, the Catholic church surely has the greatest amount of decentralization—almost to the point of anarchy sometimes (a school board and school superintendent in every parish). Similarly, as I have discussed in the chapters on the Catholic ethic and the neighborhood, the experience of American Catholics in the urban political organizations, the trade union locals, and the immigrant neighborhoods represents a very different approach to human relationships than the one to be found in the corporate bureaucracies of state capitalism or state socialism.

To be a church for the communal Catholic it is not necessary that we derive a concrete, practical program out of our own experience for the creation of a more just and human society immediately. But it is necessary to begin to think our own thoughts once again and not mindlessly repeat the fashionable cliches of others.*

A church for the communal Catholic must also be *committed*. The church can be tranquil because it believes in the power of God's love; but it must be committed because it believes that God's love demands a response. Tranquility comes from the Catholic conviction that ultimately God will provide; commitment comes from the parallel conviction that God's provision requires our cooperation. The church will tell the communal Catholic that he must labor in season and out, he can never quit, he can never permit himself to be counted out by discouragement, he can never permit himself the luxury of permanent disillusion, and he can never accept any failure as final. It will also tell him that precisely to the extent that he allows himself the time, leisure, and solitude to listen to the inspirations of the Spirit will he be able to make his commitment effectively and efficiently to be of service to the least of the brothers. Precisely because it can take the long view, a church for the communal Catholic cannot tolerate the abandonment of effort with the suffering of short-run failures no matter how discouraging and disheartening such failures may be. When a communal Catholic says that he wishes the church would calm down, he does not mean that it should cop out.

It is absolutely necessary that the Catholic church in the United States begin to recognize the value of ideas and assume once again the traditional role of the defender of Catholic civility and intellectualism. The new barbarians are at the gates, and unfortunately many of them are already inside. Through the whole long agony of our

---

*A good place to begin the development of a critique of corporate bureaucracies would be the observation that no corporate organization—capitalist or socialist—functions the way its formal organizational charts designate. Indeed, any corporate body which was held to the channels of communication established by its organizational charts would grind to a halt. Why do all organization theories, both capitalist and socialist, ignore the obvious fact that the organization functions by violating the channels of communication described by theory and delineated by organizational charts? Could it be that they have missed something important about human nature?

conflict with the Enlightenment, Catholicism had to insist there was
something more in the human condition than pure rationality. But the
Enlightenment is dead, and faith in human reason is in retreat. We
can therefore return to that traditional position which we have held
since the time of the Apostolic Fathers and begin to defend human
reason against its enemies once more.

If you wish to communicate with a communal Catholic, then appeal first of all to his intellect. Don't shout at him, rant at him, hector
him, hassle him. He is hassled by enough other people to whom he
has to listen. Since he no longer has to listen to you, he won't if you
shout at him. Let us suppose you wish to gain his sympathy for
foreign economic aid. The survey data show that he is already sympathetic to such a program. Inform him of the dangers of acute
hunger problems in certain parts of the world, with possible famine.
Detail the various analyses of the causes of the problem, explain the
solutions which seem to be available, outline the option you think
most appropriate, urge him to some kind of action. Don't tell him he
is personally responsible for the food shortage in India because he
knows he is not. Do not tell him that his giving up meat once a week
would solve the problem because he knows better. Do not preach to
him about the moral superiority of the third world, because he reads
the newspapers and knows better. Do not tell him that the hungry of
the world will rise up and destroy the rich and the well fed. He knows
that it is never the poor and the hungry that start revolutions but
rather the middle class. The more you know about international
economics, agricultural technology, different problems in different
countries, and the complexities and intricacies of food distribution,
the more he is likely to believe you. But if he discovers that you are
using your Roman collar (physically or symbolically), enthusiasm,
or Christianity as a way of obtaining a clerical discount on competence, he will switch you off and turn to another channel.

For the communal Catholic the church must also be prepared to
listen. It must not only be intellectual, it must also be sympathetic,
sensitive, and comprehending. And that is so difficult. American
Catholics learned during the era of apologetic Catholicism to have

answers. Indeed, the training we received in college religion classes and seminary theology classes was often nothing more than an endless process of memorizing answers so that we could go forth into the world equipped for an answer to every question we might be asked. The paradigmatic relationship in apologetic Catholicism was the lay person in the rectory office asking the question, and the priest reaching back in his memory for either the answer he had once learned or at least the textbook which would provide it. Bishops were expected to have the answers priests would ask, and bishops would make pilgrimages to Rome because the pope had the answers they lacked. Presumably the pope withdrew into his chapel at night to obtain answers from God to his questions.

We have abandoned this paradigm, but not its style. The questions and the answers are different, but most ecclesial Catholics still think of religious discussion (save for ecumenical dialogue with our separated brothers) as monologues in which I answer your question and vice versa. Consciousness raising is no more than a psychological, sophisticated effort to persuade others to ask the questions for which we have the answers. The answers, as I say, may be different from the old ones, but the function of the church is still the same—giving answers to questions you try to persuade others to ask. The communal Catholic says to the church in effect, "Damn it, I don't want your answers to either the old questions or the new ones. I want you to listen while I tell you what my problems are. I want you to listen because what's a church good for if it won't listen to its people?"

Humanae Vitae was the most disastrous of the contemporary exercises in nonlistening. One must say with all respect and deference that the encyclical showed that the pope had not listened to his own commission. He sketched their arguments briefly, but he did not respond to them, much less give any evidence at all that he really understood what the commissioners and the Catholic world for whom they spoke were trying to say. No one was denying the importance of human life; no one was questioning the indispensability of the human family; no one was challenging the sanctity of marriage; no one was doubting the importance or the holiness of procreation. On the contrary, life, family, marriage, and procreation were all valued as much by the commissioners and the Catholic people for whom they spoke as they were by the pope. But the overwhelming burden of the responsibility which he perceived to be his seemed to have made it impossible for the pope to really hear what they were saying. He heard the words, but he did not hear the profound human feelings that lay behind them.

Similarly, many bishops and priests did not, and do not now, really understand the agony of American minority groups. The blacks, the Latins, the American Indians—despite some of their more noisy spokesmen—do not want out of American society, they want in. Catholics, who just got in themselves, (and some not very far yet), should of all people be able to understand that. Still, all too many church leaders didn't listen; they were terrified by minority militancy. Some of the younger clergy went to the extreme of being more militant than the militants and supported a separatism that the minorities wanted less than anyone else. Many Catholic social actionists refused to believe that the people living in ethnic neighborhoods had real problems and valid fears. Uneasiness about racial change was dismissed as bigotry, and we became ashamed of our own people. Psychologist Robert Coles went into their neighborhoods and listened to them; the Catholic social actionists and sometimes even their own curates simply did not understand what they were saying.

St. Benedict told his father abbot to listen to all the monks, even the youngest. Pope John included in his motto the primary instruction, *"omne videre."* The wise and learned confessor of the Catholic myth listened 95 percent of the time and spoke very little, but there do not seem to be many Friar Lawrences around today. Until there are, until there is a church with the self-discipline, self-confidence, and self-restraint to listen and listen carefully, the communal Catholics will not listen to the church. They are unable to talk to it.

The communal Catholic has been around. He knows, as Gustav Weigel once remarked, that all human efforts, given sufficient time, go badly. He is also aware of the fragility of human nature and his own particular manifestation of it, and he cannot afford the luxury of utopia. He knows, as George Orwell has said, that all revolutions fail but that the failures are different. He does not expect the Golden Age or the New Era to begin tomorrow or the next day. He therefore expects his church to be realistic about the human prospect, about its own strengths and weaknesses, about its own frailties. The *multa dissimulare, pauca corrigere* of Pope John received a sympathetic resonance in the personality of the communal Catholic. He simply cannot abide a perfectionist church because he knows he is incapable of perfection and because, as he looks at the church, he sees how little perfection is in it. Human nature might not be very much. Loren Eiseley suggests that evolution made a horrendous mistake when it produced humankind. The communal Catholic is likely to smile when he is told that the Chinese are creating a new form of human nature. He remembered that the same thing was said about the Russians in the 1930s. A church that expects the impossible, requires the impossible, preaches the impossible, and demands the impossible is a church for archangels and Cherubim, perhaps, but not for human beings. The vow of St. Louis Grignion De Montfort to always do the more perfect thing is currently out of fashion, but there are still lots of preachers and prophets abroad in the land, of both left and right wing persuasions, who are trying to impose a vast variety of moral obligations on God's people—all serenely oblivious to the fact that Jesus came to preach not obligations but God's sympathetic, forgiving, all comprehending love.

The most important thing that a communal Catholic will require in a church to which he is prepared to listen is that it will speak to him of hope. For it is only if he has hope that he will be able to renew the struggle against discouragements, failures, and frustrations of life and the weakness, inadequacy, narrowness, and pettiness of his own personality. There may be times in life when optimism comes easy. If you are young, healthy, and vigorous, and your whole life stretches before you, then it is not hard to be an optimist; but by the time you turn thirty, the body slows down, the spirit grows weary, and death looms ever larger. Similarly, in the full blush of scientific, evolutionary Enlightenment optimism it was easy—or at least easier—to think that liberalism, democracy, rationality, and technology would solve all human problems. Now with pollution, nuclear peril, threatened world food shortage, resurgence of the proletarianism of both the left and the right, and the collapse of democracies in the new countries, one can advise humankind to become like Robert Heilbroner's Atlas and patiently bear the heavy burden of its responsibilities while waiting for Armageddon. You don't have to tell the communal Catholic that darkness is descending upon the earth. Haven't you noticed that he already has his flashlight on? Nor do you have to tell him that it's dangerous to walk the streets at night. Why do you think he has a triple lock on his door? Nor do you have to warn him about the smothering effect of corporate irresponsibility. He has an Internal Revenue Service 1040 form on his desk.

He needs to hear that there is still a little light left, and maybe, just maybe, it has grown a shade brighter. He needs to be told that on balance and all things considered human nature is a little more admirable than despicable, and that he still has within himself the power to laugh, play, love, and celebrate. He so desperately wants to hear that the family is not falling apart or becoming obsolete, but that he, his wife, and children can grow in love together. He needs to hear that it is still possible to join with other human beings in open and trusting communities. He wants to hear that the last ugly, vicious, oppressive word of death is not the final word after all. He wants to be told that after the harsh bitter cold of winter one may begin to feel the faint warm breath of spring. What the hell good is a church that does not preach hope?

A church for the communal Catholic must be mature. Like everyone else in the world, the communal Catholic is only intermittently an adult; but when he goes to his church, he expects to be treated like an adult and deal with people who are capable of acting like adults. The last thing in the world he needs in this church is leadership that is hung up on authority. The church, of course, has no monopoly on authoritarianism or authority hang-ups, as five minutes of experience in any other large corporate bureaucracy will make clear. Humankind has not yet shaken the Oedipus complex. The fixation on father figures and mother figures in the church is so obvious, so pervasive, and so utterly degrading that the communal Catholic is quickly turned off. He observes that priests, religious, and a certain kind of lay person can talk about virtually nothing else but their bishop or "the bishops"; but they are quite incapable of doing anything about authority. If he has any psychological sophistication at all, the communal Catholic may conclude that many ecclesial Catholic confreres desperately need father figures or mother figures both to lean on and hate.

Nor is he very edified with a group of priests or religious obsessed with authority relationships who yet respond to organizational problems by making rules, which of course only serve to increase the already heavy authority structure. In my own archdiocese, the priests' senate was faced with a problem: there was a shortage of volunteers for inner-city work. There were some parishes to which no one wanted to be sent. How did they solve the problem? Did they try to find root causes for the problem and eliminate those causes? Did they try to discover what was unattractive about inner-city parishes or certain other assignments and modify the structure of such assignments? Hardly. They made two rules: you could only serve in a parish for five years, and everyone had to expect in their career at least one assignment in the inner city. It was neat, orderly, efficient, and authoritarian as all hell. A communal Catholic who observed such an immature and childish response to a serious problem might be excused for saying that if the clergy ever grew up and learned how to deal realistically with complicated issues, then he would be happy to listen to what the clergy had to say. But little children, or those who deal with little children, solve problems by making rules. Grown-ups don't. There is enough immaturity in the world in which the communal Catholic lives. He sees no reason why he should have to put up with it in his church too.

The communal Catholic does not want a church that is childish, but he would find one attractive that occasionally demonstrated some capacity to be childlike. There are not many things in life worth celebrating, and after awhile, it turns out, not very many things worth getting enthusiastic about either. Someone who is a playful enthusiast at seventeen is behaving the way a seventeen-year-old should; someone who is playful and enthusiastic at forty is either crazy or has discovered the secret of life. A church which can be mature, realistic, sophisticated, and rational, and *still* be incorrigibly playful, joyous, and enthusiastic is a church of either madmen or saints. And while you may not want to join such a crowd at first, you will at least find them attractive and want to learn more about them.

My sister, Mary Durkin, in her book *The Suburban Women*, has a melancholy passage (or so it seemed to me) about her youngest daughter, Elizabeth (alias "Little Bit") and the joyous song she sang as a four-year-old. "Now," the author notes, "Elizabeth is in school, and school has dimmed her joy somewhat." My sister's point is that Elizabeth's joy is Christian, and any other response to life is non-Christian. Her rueful acceptance of the inevitable destruction of childlike joy by the oppressive bureaucracy—school—struck me as very sad. Knowing Little Bit myself, I would say that any institution that dims her joy is damnable, and if that is what schools do to the joyfulness of little children—and of course that *is* what they do—then schools ought to be destroyed, or perhaps, more moderately, drastically reformed. I think I know what the Founder had in mind when he said, "Unless you become like little children."

Humble, excellent, traditional, radical, relaxed, committed, intellectual, sensitive, realistic, hopeful, mature, and enthusiastic—such are the qualities of a church to which the communal Catholic might begin to listen. But there are three sets of arguments which could be made against the utility of this description. First of all it might be said that these characteristics already exist in the American church and are characteristic of its structure, operation, and the majority of its personnel. To those who would make this argument, I reply that they simply don't know much about the American church. It could also be argued that the qualities I have described are abstract, do not speak to specific issues, are not programmatic, and do not suggest structural reforms. To this argument I would respond that most of the problems of human life, both personal and social, do not have to do with specific issues, concrete programs, or structural forms but with the overarching theme, the fundamental character of a person or an institution. The medium is not the message, style is not substance; but both substance and style are symptoms of its fundamental character.

Finally, it could be said that my vision of the church for a communal Catholic is too ambitious, too idealistic. I have described a church without spots, without flaws, and perfection can only be expected, by my own admission, when the Bridegroom returns. Obviously, a church which rates a score of 100 on the twelve scales implicit in this chapter would be a perfect church; and just as obviously we are not likely to see such a church. But the issue is not so much achieving perfection as reordering goals and priorities, modifying emphases, and adapting procedures.

From 1800 to 1950, the fundamental goal of American Catholicism was to defend the faith of the immigrants. The character traits required for that defense were order, skill in fund-raising, discipline, and pragmatic responsiveness to the conflicting demands of different ethnic groups. These traits were developed gradually over the years. The emergence of the communal Catholic indicates that there is now a different crisis and a different challenge. To protect the faith is one challenge; to reestablish credibility, or perhaps to establish credibility in a whole new environment, is another challenge. Given the fact that most large corporate institutions—business, government, education—presently enjoy rather little credibility, the problem for the ecclesial institution is not to achieve perfect credibility but rather to do a little bit better than the opposition. It should not be an insurmountable difficulty.

Still, it is a long way from the ecclesial Catholicism of the present moment to an even minimally credible church to which the communal Catholic can turn with trust and confidence. How long will it take us to travel that distance? It should not take too long. As I have argued in previous chapters, the American church has available to itself considerable resources. There is also, perhaps left over from the pre-Vatican church, boundless (if frequently misdirected) energy. The deficiencies are not resources, energy or even sincerity. The lack is in understanding and will. The formal leadership of the ecclesial institution is not aware, or will not permit itself to be aware, of how acute its credibility problem is. The turnaround cannot begin until those who lead the church, formally and informally, become aware of the depth and dimension of their problem.

There is, of course, a perception that *something* is wrong. Church attendance is down, contributions are down (taking inflation into account); Catholic magazines, newspapers, and some publishing houses are folding. Even if the data reported in *Catholic Schools in a Changing Church* are inaccurate, no one really needs statistical evidence to know that the ecclesial institution has very serious troubles. But it is not easy to live in a time of a major historical turning point or to stand on a watershed and wonder what lies beyond. If credibility is the real cause of the crisis in the church, then drastic and dramatic changes will have to occur. Many of those in top leadership positions, for example, will either have to resign or be removed from office. Such painful changes, which would have to occur from top to bottom in the church, are distasteful, disturbing, and unpleasant. It is better to adopt the strategy of the ostrich; pretend the problem isn't there and hope it will go away eventually. The prospect is for drift, perhaps drift for a long time, maybe even for the rest of the present century. A church which will appeal to the communal Catholic will, I am convinced, eventually emerge. Its characteristics are too deeply rooted in the essence of the Catholic tradition for it not to become a reality. The question is not whether but when. Perhaps another question is, how many of the children or grandchildren of today's communal Catholics will have drifted away completely, not only from the ecclesial institution but also from the Catholic community, before the change occurs?

I do not expect to live to see a church that can talk to the communal Catholics.

I've been wrong before.